Advance Praise for *Good Mourning*

"By distinguishing between grief and mourning, this book serves the purpose of taking the reader on a journey through one's own grief, with its seemingly conflicting myriad of feelings and thoughts, gradually emerging so as to enter the process of mourning. This ritualistic process incorporates spiritual practices, integrating the loss to eventually enter a new phase of one's life. This is the transformative journey, according to Dr. Cole, which links our suffering with the suffering of God, as we give our pain to God and rely on the healing presence of the Holy Spirit. I highly recommend this book as a guide and devotional resource for the grief-stricken soul. I also found it to be a comprehensive, in-depth treatment of grief and mourning, which should be included in the library of every caregiver, whether lay or professional."
—David R. Jenkins, DMin, Director of Chaplaincy
M. D. Anderson Cancer Center, the University of Texas

"Military chaplains and all ministers who serve congregations affected by war will want this book. This one volume is essential both as a gift to the bereaved and for Bible study groups. Allan Cole provides a masterful perspective on how to mourn and how to interpret suffering. His spiritual practices for those who mourn are a must-read for all pastoral care providers."
—Lieutenant Colonel David Scheider, Episcopal Priest, a member
of the American Association of Pastoral Counselors, Diplomate

"Grief is a messy, disorienting, and demoralizing experience. For those in deep or prolonged grief, Professor Cole's words provide just the right guidance: humane, well-informed, and profoundly reasonable. Instead of finding the usual superficialities of most self-help books, readers will discover a respect for the depth of their pain and a well-lit path through the grieving process."
—Daniel Morehead, MD, Private Practice and Consulting
Psychiatrist, Supervising Psychiatrist for Samaritan Center
for Counseling and Pastoral Care, Austin, Texas

"Both sane and spiritual, this book is a godsend for those who are experiencing grief—and for all those who love or work with them."

—Greg Garrett, Professor of English at Baylor University, Writer-in-Residence at Episcopal Theological Seminary, and author of *The Gospel according to Hollywood, Stories from the Edge,* and *Holy Superheroes! Revised and Expanded Edition: Exploring the Sacred in Comics, Graphic Novels, and Film*

"*Good Mourning* is a must-read for anyone who has experienced a significant loss. This book is a valuable resource for every social worker and pastoral counselor to use with the bereaved. In this easy-to-read book, Dr. Allan Cole provides a sound, conceptual framework for understanding grief and mourning and the blueprints for how to cope with common emotional and behavioral reactions experienced during loss. *Good Mourning* is filled with practical strategies and experiential exercises that guide readers on how to rebuild their lives during the mourning process. This book is most impressive. It combines the best resources from both behavioral sciences and theology to help people cope with grief and to transform their lives during times of significant loss."

—Cynthia Franklin, PhD, LCSW, LMFT, Stiernberg/Spencer Family Professor in Mental Health, the University of Texas at Austin School of Social Work

Good Mourning

Other books by Allan Hugh Cole Jr.
from Westminster John Knox Press

Losers, Loners, and Rebels: The Spiritual Struggles of Boys
(with Robert C. Dykstra and Donald Capps)

Good Mourning

Getting through Your Grief

ALLAN HUGH COLE JR.

Westminster John Knox Press
LOUISVILLE • LONDON

Scripture quotations from the New Revised Standard Version of the Bible are copyright © 1989 by the Division of Christian Education of the National Council of the Churches of Christ in the U.S.A. and are used by permission.

Excerpt from "Words about Grief" in *Collected Poems* by Elizabeth Jennings (New York: Carcanet, 1986) is reprinted by permission of David Higham Associates. All rights reserved.

Book design by Sharon Adams
Cover design by Eric Walljasper, Minneapolis, MN

First edition
Published by Westminster John Knox Press
Louisville, Kentucky

This book is printed on acid-free paper that meets the American National Standards Institute Z39.48 standard. ∞

PRINTED IN THE UNITED STATES OF AMERICA

08 09 10 11 12 13 14 15 16 17 — 10 9 8 7 6 5 4 3 2 1

Library of Congress Cataloging-in-Publication Data

Cole, Allan Hugh.
    Good mourning : getting through your grief / Allan Hugh Cole, Jr.—1st ed.
      p. cm.
   ISBN 978-0-664-23268-9 (alk. paper)
    1. Grief—Religious aspects—Christianity. 2. Bereavement—Religious aspects—Christianity. 3. Loss (Psychology)—Religious aspects—Christianity. I. Title.
   BV4905.3.C645 2008
   248.8'66—dc22

2007045709

For my parents,
Allan and Jeri Cole

Contents

Preface

As a professor of pastoral care, I am asked often to suggest a good book for someone who has suffered a significant loss. Requests come from students, ministers, colleagues, church members, family members, friends, and neighbors. Sometimes they want to read the book themselves. More often, they want someone they care about to read it. Either way, they seek assistance with getting through grief, dealing with sorrow, or a related goal having to do with the hole in someone's life produced by an experience of loss.

I attribute these frequent requests to the persistent nature of loss. Sooner or later it touches all of us. Some people experience a multitude of losses. Most of us know individuals or families for whom one loss after another has occurred. We may find ourselves saying about these persons: "How much more can they take?" or "I cannot imagine dealing with what they have." Others may experience loss with less frequency, but loss is a part of life for us all. As a result, most of us want to enlist whatever help we can for getting through our losses and helping others get through theirs.

Other factors inform requests for a good book on loss. When we sustain a loss, some of us want and need to *reflect* on what has occurred. We want to understand our experience of loss. We need to think about what has been lost. We want to think about how to push ahead and live with the absence of what we love. Perhaps we also need to do any or all of this at our own pace and on our own terms. We want to approach dealing with loss in a way that feels like a good fit with respect to where we are, who we are, and what we deem distinctive about ourselves, our experiences, and our needs. Reading a book on loss can help.

At the same time, some of us want ways of dealing with loss that don't *necessarily* involve talking about it with others, at least not immediately or in an extended way. I have in mind here those who are reluctant to join "grief recovery" groups or to engage in "grief therapy." But I also have in mind those who are not inclined to share their painful experiences with family members, friends, close associates, or even their minister—at least not for the time being. Sometimes we need to begin a journey of getting through loss more or less alone. We want to get oriented on the highway of loss before committing to travel across its long miles, especially with a companion. A good book on loss can help with this orientation.

For some, reading a good book on loss can provide sufficient support. A book helps them gain perspective on their experiences and inspires what needs to occur in order to "get through" loss. For most of us, though, a good book on loss will be the impetus for securing additional helps and resources. These might include a support group, in-depth counseling, or intentional conversations with a minister or other caregiver. But while many of us will benefit from sharing painful experiences with others at some point, how and when this happens will vary from person to person.

We may read a book on loss in conjunction with other supports. In fact, a multifaceted approach may best provide what most of us need. Whatever approach you feel is best for you, however, I hope that this book will help you live with your loss and experience personal, relational, and spiritual growth along the way.

Acknowledgments

In the spring of 2007, I enjoyed a dinner of Mexican food in Austin, Texas, with Jon Berquist, executive editor for biblical studies at Westminster John Knox Press. Jon and I discussed various projects of interest and how we might work together to develop them. The idea for this book was Jon's. It's written for those who have experienced a significant loss themselves and for those who seek to help them. It's a book aimed at helping those who have sustained a loss to experience "good mourning." I remain grateful for Jon's vision, advice, and friendship. Every scholar should have the good fortune of working with someone like him. I am also thankful for the support offered by Julie Tonini, managing editor at Westminster John Knox Press. She is the epitome of efficiency and precision.

Several people who are both colleagues and friends gave generous amounts of time and energy to read this book's manuscript. These include Donald Capps, Robert Dykstra, David Jensen, David Lee Jones, Duane Bidwell, Janet Maykus, and Henry Summerall. Their wisdom and insights helped me say what I wanted to say better, even when they would have said it differently or not said it at all.

I would be remiss without acknowledging as well the influence of J. William Worden on my thinking about mourning. Imprints of his "four tasks of mourning" are found throughout this book.

I enjoy the privilege of teaching, learning, writing, and living in the Austin Presbyterian Theological Seminary community. I know of no place more conducive to creative learning and work. My faculty colleagues, our students, and the seminary's administration and staff enhance many lives—my own included—and certainly bring joy to my chosen vocation. I am especially grateful to President Ted Wardlaw and Dean Michael Jinkins for encouraging faculty development and working with diligence to provide for it.

My wife, Tracey, and our two daughters, Meredith and Holly, provide countless blessings, boundless joy, and constant reminders of the gifts of love and a life shared. Tracey, a gifted social worker, generously gave the time and energy required to read this book's manuscript and offered thoughtful feedback, too, just prior to giving birth to Holly. My parents, Allan and Jeri Cole, have offered devotion and support throughout my life and have taught me and many others much about caring. Donald Capps and Robert C. Dykstra continue to teach me by their examples. They model the best in scholarship, collegiality, and friendship. Finally, Tony Genosa, Robert Drago, Karen Shore, Daniel Morehead, and Deborah Shelton are special friends and confidants who have listened to quips, queries, and quandaries surrounding my own losses and encouraged good mourning.

Introduction

If you are reading this book, you are probably grieving a significant loss. Perhaps your parent, spouse, child, partner, or other loved one has died or has a severe illness. Maybe your marriage or another significant relationship has ended. Possibly you have realized that conceiving a child or parenting a healthy child will not be in your future. Perhaps you have discovered that embarking on a particular vocation, ascending to the heights of your profession, or some other long-held dream is now impossible to fulfill. You might have lost a job that you loved and that gave you a deep sense of purpose. Maybe you have become aware of your declining ability to function physically, intellectually, or creatively. Or you have moved from your familiar surroundings and roots, and you now experience strange environments or routines. Perhaps you have had some other kind of loss. You find yourself living in a strange new world marked by the absence of what you loved and lost. You need support, understanding, and guidance as you try to get your bearings. You want help for finding your way through grief. This book seeks to provide some aid.

THE NATURE OF LOSS

Each human being experiences loss uniquely. We find similarities across people's experiences, but no person's grief unfolds exactly like another's. As in an experience of love, we encounter loss in ways that become distinctly our own. My grief is mine. Your grief is yours. Joe's grief is his own, too. Each of us will encounter grief in our own way. Still, it's tempting to try to quantify our losses or grief experiences and compare them to those of others.

We easily find ourselves engaging in such comparisons. For example, witnessing a friend sobbing at a funeral service while the rest of her family members remain more or less composed, we assume that our friend grieves more intensely than the rest of her family. We might also assume that our friend loved the deceased person more than the others did, and will miss the deceased more than they will. But these assumptions may be misguided. We all grieve in our own ways. A person who sobs may not feel any more pain than a person who appears composed. Similarly, a person who laughs as she tells stories about her loved one may hurt and grieve just as much as the person who remains quiet and appears rather stoic. People grieve differently. It's true that we can support and learn from one another by sharing our experiences. At the same time, assuming too much commonality among the bereaved leads to neglecting the uniqueness of each person's experience. This neglect does injustice to and further injures already hurting persons.

The need to avoid quantifying or comparing grief experiences also holds when considering various losses experienced by the same person. Sometimes people wonder why one experience of loss seems so different from another. Often they begin to speculate about why they are not coping as well this time, or, instead, why they are not having a harder time on this occasion, given how difficult the previous loss was for them. They compare their multiple experiences of loss, assuming that each one calls for a similar response.

But just as different people grieve differently, any one of us may respond in a different manner from one loss to another. Numerous factors influence our responses. These include what or whom we have lost, how the loss occurred, the nature of our relationship to the loss, and other variables relating to our physical, emotional, relational, economic, and spiritual states. So it's worth keeping in mind that different people grieve in different ways, but that the same people grieve in different ways too. One loss does not necessarily feel like another.

Our differences notwithstanding, these words from the poet Elizabeth Jennings capture the essence of loss for many of us.

Time does not heal,
It makes a half-stitched scar
That can be broken and you feel
Grief as total as in its first hour.[1]

Losing someone or something significant leaves a lasting scar. Its state of healing remains uncertain. Occasionally, this scar reopens to expose a painful wound of absence that accompanies us through life. This poem recognizes that loss lasts a long time and its effects accumulate. Losses stay with us. They take hold of us and can influence how we experience life. Losses affect our relationships, hopes for the future, and the risks that we are willing to take. We can learn to live in the midst of loss with a degree of peace and acceptance, but it is very rare to "get over" a significant loss. Why? Because losses leave "half-stitched" scars that mark us emotionally, relationally, physically, and spiritually. Newly experienced losses can lance scars left by previous losses. These previous losses may prompt us to feel the rawness of present losses more severely and persistently than we would otherwise.

A friend of mine experienced the effects that previous losses can have on present ones when his cousin committed suicide. As my friend describes the experience, "One morning not long after my cousin died, as I read the Bible and prayed, out of nowhere I began weeping and big hot tears started falling on the page. It shocked me because my cousin and I were never close; he was twenty years younger. But then I realized that the tears were not just for him. His death was only the trigger. My tears were really for my father and brother and sister who had died, and whose deaths I had not mourned in a healthy way."

Another example of how present losses can reawaken previous ones is when a person experiences the loss of a marriage through divorce after having experienced the loss of a parent years before. The grief experienced over the divorce is itself substantial. But it worsens due to the emotional residue left by the previous loss (the death of a parent) that has not yet been mourned. The scar from the loss of the parent opens because of the lost marriage, which leaves its own lasting scar. One grief counselor, Dorothy S. Becvar, has characterized the result of the cumulative scars that losses deposit. We need to learn to live "in the presence of grief."[2]

Another poet, Anne Sexton, offers the image of a "dead heart" to describe what it feels like to suffer loss. For many grievers, and perhaps for you, this dead heart resides strangely inside, injured and unpredictable. It can fashion you into a stranger, to yourself and others. I have written this book for anyone whose *own* heart feels as if it is dying. It is a book for those sporting scars in body, mind, or spirit that have formed, opened, or reopened because of loss.

The loss of someone or something significant produces predictable responses. These include feelings of sadness, anxiety, fear, anger, hopelessness, frustration, guilt or regret, exhaustion, loneliness, relief, and yearning for what we no longer have in our lives. We may also notice that loss affects how we think. Loss generates shock and disbelief, confusion, memory loss, and an inability to concentrate. Loss can impact the ability to sleep, and it can result in frequent dreams or nightmares having to do with what we have lost. Sustaining a loss can also affect how we behave. We may find it difficult to communicate with others or get along with them. Or we discover that following loss we withdraw from significant relationships, devote less energy to work or work-related matters, or spend less time on hobbies and other passions.

Losses can affect us physically, too. They can cause nausea, a sensation of emptiness inside, heart palpitations, jitteriness, dizziness, and exhaustion. In more severe cases, loss may trigger the inability to feel altogether. This is the menacing nature of loss. It can rob us of the ability to feel. In these cases, the "dead heart" numbs us to life and, with this, to love and hope. Finding yourself with this kind of heart can make you fear that it will never live again. This fear makes the struggle with grief even more severe.

Time alone will not heal grief, as Elizabeth Jennings suggests in her poem. Still, what we experience during the passing of time after a loss has much to do with our health, wholeness, and vitality. How we consider our losses, approach living with them, and what we do or refrain from doing in their aftermath matters a great deal. Our responses to loss affect the extent to which we find relief from the "totality" of our pain. We may learn to respond to loss in ways that keep our scars intact and minimize the frequency and degree to which our wounds are exposed as we travel the never-ending path of life after loss.

BEREAVEMENT, GRIEF, AND MOURNING

It is useful to distinguish between three terms associated with experiences of loss: *bereavement*, *grief*, and *mourning*. Although these terms get used interchangeably, each has a distinct meaning.

Bereavement is the most general of these three terms. It refers to the fact that one has experienced a significant loss. When we identify someone as bereaved, we mean that she lives with the absence of what she once loved or valued. She lives on "this side" of a loss. Bereavement serves as an umbrella term that simply notes the occurrence of loss. It offers little in the way of specifics.

Grief, on the other hand, refers to something more specific. It describes the various painful and complex psychological, emotional, physical, spiritual, behavioral, and relational responses to loss that one endures. Typical grief responses include a whole host of feelings, thoughts, behaviors, spiritual or religious questions, relational challenges, and many stressors. To say that we grieve means that a loss has occurred, but also that we are responding to that loss in noticeable ways. These responses are expected and natural. We *need* to grieve when we lose someone or something important to us. Grieving prepares us for mourning.

Mourning proceeds from an experience of grief. As will become clear, we need to grieve before we can mourn. I will use the term *mourning* to refer to the process by which a bereaved person gradually changes her relationship to what has been lost, so that an emotional investment in new relationships and other aspects of life may occur. Mourning describes the manner of getting through loss over time. Mourning certainly involves continued grieving, but the mourning process also involves learning how to live with a lasting void created by what we have lost.

None of us looks forward to the loss of what we love. But given the fact that these losses occur, we do well to think about how best to live with them. Even if we don't get over losses completely, we can learn to live more at peace in their presence. The mourning process provides for this peace. But mourning does not happen by itself. It must be sought and intentionally engaged. I would even say that mourning requires active pursuit. It takes energy, effort, focus, and yes, hard work to experience good mourning.

ABOUT THIS BOOK

This book provides straight talk about grief—the ways people experience loss. It likewise focuses on specific strategies for moving through losses in ways that foster physical, emotional, relational, and spiritual benefits. This process of moving through losses is called *mourning*. The book's title, *Good Mourning*, indicates that mourning is in fact good or desirable. When we sustain a significant loss, we need to mourn it. Mourning our losses is a worthy goal.

One way that we can experience "good" mourning is to mourn well. What does mourning well mean? It means at least two things. First, mourning can occur with greater or lesser "benefits." By this I mean an outcome marked by a measure of health, wholeness, renewed faith and hope, and overall well-being that lends support for living with loss. We may mourn well or not so well, in helpful or unhelpful ways.

"Mourning well" also suggests the image of a fount or wellspring—a source of life, perhaps—that we may tap for renewal. So "mourning" invites us to look within ourselves for what we need to sustain us as we try to continue living. Part 1 pays particular attention to how, on the one hand, we may look within ourselves to grasp the effects of loss and determine what we need to move through it. On the other hand, the principal "life source" that we need to tap in mourning is God and what God promises to provide. Recall Jesus' words to the Samaritan woman as they stood beside a well of water: "Everyone who drinks of this water will be thirsty again, but those who drink of the water that I will give them will never be thirsty. The water that I will give will become in them a spring of water gushing up to eternal life" (John 4:13–14). This book will encourage you to discover ways for tapping the wellspring that God provides.

You might want to view this book as demonstrating the "good" in mourning by focusing on how to mourn in ways that benefit you. This is the first connotation of "mourning well." But the book also suggests how to tap the divine source of repair or renewal, the second connotation of "mourning well." This wellspring of life is *your* mourning well. It will sustain you through loss.

The book's subtitle, "Getting through Your Grief," indicates that how we approach mourning, or the "strategies" employed to get through our grief, has much to do with the benefits we discover. We foster our "mourning well" (benefits) and draw most efficiently from our "mourning well" (God as the source of life) by first considering the "what" of grief. The "what" of grief asks questions like: What makes loss so difficult? What effect does loss have on us? What helps us cope with loss in ways that lead to good mourning? Part 1 attends to these "what" questions.

But then we need to ask the "so what?" questions of mourning. These "so what?" questions include: How do I find the strength to go on? How do I begin to put my life back together? Will I ever love again? Can I ever be happy again? To answer these "so what?" questions, in part 2 we consider what mourning requires, what promotes "good" mourning, and what role faith and prayer can play in mourning well.

A focus on the "what" of grief (part 1) considers typical grief responses, so that we understand what usually happens when we suffer loss. Greater understanding will help you map your own experience. It may shed light on what to expect as you go forward. Understanding also helps you feel less troubled by your seemingly odd and unanticipated thoughts, feelings, and behaviors that accompany grief. A focus on the "so what?" accompanying loss (part 2) will help you consider ways to encourage good mourning and discover answers to the kinds of questions previously cited. These mourning strategies will help you navigate your way through loss in healthier and more faithful ways.

HOW TO USE THIS BOOK

It may be best to wait a few months after your loss to read this book. Why? Because it usually takes a few months of grieving before we are prepared to mourn. For most people, this process takes time. Initially following a loss, we feel shocked, confused, disoriented, angry, unsettled, and a host of other feelings. These experiences demand so much from us that we have little energy left to give to matters beyond our most basic needs. In other words, for the first few days and weeks following a significant loss, we usually lack the energy, focus, and desire required for mourning. We benefit, therefore, from giving ourselves some time for "finding our bearings" or "waking back up to life." In order to mourn well, grief needs its own time, attention, and focus.

If, however, you happen to be reading this book before the three-month mark, I would encourage you to read it again after a few more months have passed. Wherever you may be in the journey through loss, you can benefit from repetition with regard to the strategies I have suggested. It may even be helpful to reread the book every few months for the first year or two after your loss. Though this may sound like a lot of work, this repetitive reading will likely benefit you as you mourn.

Keep in mind, too, that you need not read this book in a single sitting, or two or three sittings. It may prove most beneficial to read a chapter or two at a time, sit with it for a while, and then return to read more. Or perhaps it will be most beneficial to read the same chapter or chapters more than once before moving on to the next one. There is no rush to get through the book.

FINDING BLESSINGS IN MOURNING

In the Sermon on the Mount, Jesus spoke of blessings in mourning. He said: "Blessed are those who mourn, for they will be comforted" (Matt. 5:4). Jesus recognizes the inseparable link between mourning and comfort. We find comfort to the extent that we mourn. Mourning well and the comfort that this provides is what God desires for our lives. Mourning is no easy task. In fact, there may be nothing more difficult than truly mourning a significant loss. So much in the culture around us tends to minimize our experiences of loss, and thus our need for mourning. Some people, usually well-intentioned, may urge you to "get on with life" and "get over it" just as you begin experiencing the intense pain associated with your loss. Responses like these may serve to make an already demanding journey even more difficult.

Embarking on a mourning journey requires a voyage into our deepest fears and uncertainties. It also invites us to encounter our foremost sources of trust and hope. But we often find these sources by daring first to discover and live with our fears and uncertainties. As you embark on the next phase of your own journey through loss, remember Jesus' assurance that this journey, however lonely and treacherous, is the only path finally to comfort and blessing. "Blessed are those who mourn, for they will be comforted," he tells us. May this be so for you!

Part 1

What?—Experiencing Loss

Like vinegar on a wound is one who sings songs to a heavy heart. Like a moth in clothing or a worm in wood, sorrow gnaws at the human heart.

Proverbs 25:20

How long must I bear pain in my soul, and have sorrow in my heart all day long?

Psalm 13:2

The eager fate which carried thee
Took the largest part of me:
For this losing is true dying;
This is lordly man's down-lying,
This his slow but sure reclining,
Star by star his world resigning.
    Ralph Waldo Emerson, *Poems*

1

What Makes Loss So Difficult?

Why must we suffer loss? This may be one of the oldest questions that people have asked. Who among us has not imagined a world where loss never occurred? Who has not dreamed of a life where we did not have to endure when what we love leaves us or is taken away? Sometimes this question of why we face losses takes on a religious or spiritual tone. We wonder why God could not have made life so that we forgo loss and keep all that we cherish forever. The writer of Ecclesiastes provides a partial answer. He assures us that "for everything there is a season, and a time for every matter under heaven: a time to be born, and a time to die . . . a time to weep, and a time to laugh; a time to mourn, and a time to dance" (3:1, 2, 4). Joined to the rhythm of life in its various seasons, somehow loss fits with the divine realm, just like "every matter under heaven."

But anyone who has suffered a profound loss will likely balk at the notion that accepting life's seasons comes naturally or easily. The question of *why* life's seasons unfold as they do, and especially why we sustain losses in the various seasons of life, remains at the forefront. We may never find sufficient answers to every question relating to why we suffer loss. But these are valid questions and we should ask them, and sometimes we find answers. At the same time, however, the Christian faith provides hope for living with unanswered questions. As we live with our questions and await answers, we benefit from a fuller understanding of the experience of loss, and especially what makes loss so difficult.

OUR CAPACITY FOR RELATIONSHIP

When thinking about why we grieve and why loss hurts so much we need to recognize two traits that all of us share. First, we have the capacity for love, affection, and devotion to others. We form attachments or bonds to people and things. This begins at birth and continues throughout life. We form our first attachments to parents and others in our immediate family. These people constitute our first life environment and interpersonal world, conveying what the world is like. As we mature, our attachments multiply. They extend beyond the immediate family to take in the larger world. We form a wider array of connections to various people and environments. These connections continue to link us with life and the world around us. Psychologists sometimes use the terms "attachment figure" or "object" to indicate what we attach ourselves to in these ways.

The figures or objects to which we become attached throughout life include other people. These may be living or deceased, and may consist of individuals, groups, or larger communities of people. We attach ourselves to parents, children, and other family members. We also form attachments to friends, colleagues, teachers, schoolmates, neighbors, team members, and ministers and those in our faith communities. Our strongest attachments, or *primary* attachments, involve those with whom we feel most closely connected in life. Typical examples include spouses, children, parents, partners, and also our closest friends.

But we also form strong attachments with animals, and particular places, regions, and countries. We find ourselves drawn to various hobbies and activities that provide a deep sense of joy and satisfaction. Likewise, we become attached to a host of other things that bestow a sense of meaning, purpose, or identity. These include our role or status in the family, at work, or in a community, church, club, or other group to which we belong. Our vocation, job, or career also bestows meaning, purpose, and identity. So, too, do our life dreams, plans for the future, religious faith, political ideals, and whatever else that informs what we value and who we understand ourselves to be.

Regardless of its object, every attachment that we form has something in common. Each attachment provides for what we desire and need most in life. These desires and needs include love and affection, physical closeness to others, social and relational benefits, and a sense of being valued as we also find value in others. These attachments provide as well for our sense of safety and security.[1] They serve as the basis for feeling that life is sufficiently predictable and benevolent. They also help us understand who we are, giving us a sense of self.

When the bonds to our significant attachments are threatened or cut, we feel less safe and secure. We feel less confident in the benevolence of life and the world around us. We may even feel that we have lost a part of ourselves. An experience of loss, therefore, touches our very core. Although any significant loss generates the pain and suffering of grief, the losses causing the most severe pain involve our strongest attachments. Our most important relationships, marked by the deepest investments of affection, bring about the most intense grief. The first trait common to all of us, and a reason that we grieve what we lose, is that we inherently form attachments that provide us with what we need most in life.

SOONER OR LATER, WE EXPERIENCE LOSS

A second trait common to human beings is that we suffer loss. At some point in our lives, loss visits us all. Eventually, we face separation from people or things that we are attached to. When this happens, we lose pleasure and the sense of safety, security, and meaning that we have enjoyed.

We usually think of loss foremost in terms of the death of a loved person. For most people this is the definitive form of loss that causes the most severe pain. But keep in mind that we experience loss in all sorts of ways throughout life. Our loss may have nothing to do with a physical death, and yet it feels as if a death has occurred. We benefit from enlarging our perception of loss by considering the various ways that it occurs. Whether a loss has to do with significant persons or other things that we cherish and value, it can inflict untold pain. Understanding the extensive nature of loss helps us to recognize various types of losses as they come our way. Recognizing them, we may better anticipate and prepare for the struggles that they bring.

WHAT IF WE DID NOT EXPERIENCE LOSS?

What if we did not suffer losses in life? Has this question ever occurred to you? Most of us have imagined a life without loss, where we did not have to endure the absence of what we love. We may imagine this kind of life just as we experience a significant loss ourselves, or as we prepare for one. As a young child, I wondered why my beloved dog could not just live forever. In college, when my maternal grandfather died rather suddenly, I had the same feeling. I remember thinking, "Wouldn't life be best if we never had to say 'goodbye' to our loved ones? Why does it have to be like this?" I now realize that in both cases I was wrestling with the loss of what I loved before I was ready to let it go. You may have had similar experiences. Perhaps you feel this way now and are pondering questions like these.

We may tell ourselves that these questions indicate an immature way of thinking. After all, as we grow up we expect to acquire greater understanding and insight about all sorts of matters by learning to think "rationally" and "realistically." As we discover early in life, adulthood requires acceptance of what is real, unpleasant though it may be. We learn that although imagination and fantasy have their place in childhood, grown-ups need to leave these behind for the "reality" of life. We may assume, therefore, that imagining a life without loss is futile if not downright silly.

Several years ago, a member of a congregation I served as pastor revealed that she lived with this assumption. A year after her husband's death, she sometimes found herself daydreaming that he was alive and with her forever. She would return home from an afternoon of various tasks and momentarily expect to see her husband sitting in his familiar chair. She wanted him back. She longed for life to be as it used to be. One day at the church, she recalled a recent occasion of this daydreaming. Telling me about it, she paused for an instant and said to herself, "Oh, grow up!" She added, "I'm such a baby." Nothing about her experience was immature or unusual. I tried to encourage her to believe this. I told her that most of us engage in this kind of wishful thinking after a loss. But she was embarrassed to discover in my presence that she was longing for her husband. She had learned that this sort of thinking belonged in the realm of fantasy. It was childish and unacceptable.

When we suffer losses, it is common to move back and forth from reality to fantasy, from rational thought to imagination. We often blur the lines between them. Theologian Nicholas Wolterstorff recounts an experience like this as it related to the death of his twenty-five-year-old son, Eric, in a hiking accident. As Wolterstorff describes his loss,

"Imagination and thought are out of phase. Sometimes it's as if he's not dead, just away. I see him. Then thought intervenes and says, 'Remember, he's dead now.' For twenty-five years I have been imagining what he's doing. That keeps on going. In me now there is this strange flux of spontaneously picturing him and then painfully reminding myself."[2]

As we learn more about grief and mourning, we discover the value in responses like Wolterstorff's and the one my former parishioner experienced. Far from being immature, silly, or otherwise inappropriate, responses like these play a protective role. When we live with both reality and fantasy, moving back and forth between what we know to be real and what we imagine or wish for, we allow ourselves to experience the real in "partial" terms. To live only partly in reality, especially in the first moments, days, and weeks after a loss, allows us some control over the degree of pain that we feel. Straddling the line between fantasy and reality allows the pain of grief to creep in slowly and in smaller doses that we may be more able to tolerate and accept. One way to prevent pain from overwhelming us is to imagine a different, less painful situation or world. Better yet, as I will suggest, we may benefit from traveling to that "unreal" world on occasion for a break from the pain of loss.

This kind of imagining offers another benefit. It prompts us to remind ourselves of what would be at stake if we did *not* experience loss. A life without loss would require a life without love. In order to escape the pain of loss, we would have to cease making an emotional investment in people and a whole host of things that matter to us and bring great joy. We would then cease to love. Living without loss would require never running the risk of loss because we opted to have nothing to lose. This would prove to be no life at all.

2

What Effect Does Loss Have on How We Feel?

How do people respond to loss? How does loss make us *feel*? Experiences of loss usually make us feel strange, perhaps in ways we have never felt before. Sometimes, just knowing that what we go through lines up with what others go through relieves our sense of feeling odd and lessens other types of pain associated with our loss. The adage "misery loves company" comes to mind here. When we experience pain, we seek solidarity with others. We seek solidarity not because we want others to hurt as we do, but because we don't want to be alone in our own suffering. Perhaps knowing that many others have gone through what we are going through in similar ways itself proves comforting.

People grieve in different ways. Grief involves a complex set of feelings, so every grief experience takes its own unique path. As you consider various ways that people grieve, it may be helpful to focus your attention specifically on how *you* are feeling, in *your* grief. Knowing about others' experiences may prove helpful. But it is more important to attend foremost to *yourself* and *your* loss. If in order to mourn we first have to grieve, you can grieve most beneficially when you concentrate on the particulars of your own experience.

HOW ARE YOU FEELING?

Begin by asking yourself, How do I feel? At first, this may seem unnecessary and undesirable. Perhaps you already have a clear sense of how you feel, namely, some form of "awful." Run the risk of asking this question anyway. Remember that in asking it we often gain more insight into how we feel. This added insight sets the stage for good mourning because we know more confidently what our experience involves and what getting through it may require.

Here is an example. You may feel "awful" after being fired from a job. Many of us will use a term like "awful" to describe painful experiences. But by exploring your feelings further, and trying to name them more exactly, you may discover new and important details about your experience. As a result, you may identify more of what you need in order to get through the awful occasion and feel better.

Perhaps you realize that the awfulness relates closely to feelings of sadness and regret, as opposed to anger and resentment. It helps to distinguish between these common, yet different, grief responses, all of which can seem "awful." Why? Because feeling sad and regretful after a loss usually arises from different experiences and creates different needs than feeling angry and resentful. More clarity on these different ways of feeling "awful" allows for deeper insight into the nature of your experience and what you require going forward. As a result, you may discern where your focus should be and where to place your energy as you grieve and mourn.

In this case, you might decide to revisit matters that you feel regretful about. To the extent that you can do this, it may help you grieve with more authenticity and better prepare you for mourning. One way to revisit feelings of regret could involve examining how you erred or neglected to fulfill responsibilities at work. This approach could help specify what you did, or failed to do, that contributed to problems there. Such an examination also may help prevent similar mistakes in the future.

Another way to address feelings of regret could involve making apologies to persons you injured, mistreated, or otherwise disappointed. You may not be able to make amends. Your efforts are not likely to resecure your job. But attempting to right your situation may relieve feelings of regret and allow you to grieve with more benefit.

COMMON FEELINGS ASSOCIATED WITH GRIEF

Grief may involve feelings of shock, numbness, sadness, depression, anger, frustration, impatience, anxiety, fear, loneliness, vulnerability, helplessness, fatigue, exhaustion, hopelessness, regret, guilt, shame, ambivalence, apathy, relief, and a greater sense of connection to, and value and yearning for, what we no longer have as part of our lives. The feelings that come with grief may take a physical form, too. An experience of grief may not include every one of these feelings, and your grief experience may include feelings not mentioned here. You are invited to reflect on the more common grief-related feelings described below, in light of your own experience, asking yourself, How do I feel?

Shock and numbness. Many people experience shock after a loss. Sometimes this shock joins with an enveloping sense of numbness. In fact, these are the most common initial feelings that accompany loss. You feel dazed and even paralyzed by what has occurred. The proverbial rug has been jerked out from under you. Tumbling to the ground, you feel stuck there, flat on your back and unable to move.

Cases of sudden or unexpected loss are most likely to induce intense experiences of shock, numbness, and related responses. This is why the news of a sudden death, such as a heart attack, suicide, or drowning, or learning of a spouse's affair, or receiving word of a loved one's terminal illness "out of the blue" usually stuns us. When we have no time to anticipate or prepare ourselves for sustaining a loss, we usually receive it with greater feelings of shock and numbness.

Nevertheless, *any* loss, including ones foreseen, may cause these feelings because *all* losses catch us off guard to some extent. We can never know exactly how a loss will affect us. As much as we try to anticipate our losses, ready ourselves for their impact, and envision what life will be like when they occur, rarely does this prepare us completely for the pain and struggle to come. Following a loss we hear people say things like "I'm just so shocked by his death" or "I don't know what to say, I'm baffled by her leaving me" or "I've never been so taken aback by anything before."

In some cases, losses have an anesthetizing effect. They rob us of an ability to feel altogether. People are referring to this numbing experience when they say things like "I feel dead to the world" or "This has left me feeling frozen, like nothing will ever matter again." Whatever the degree of preparedness, any loss may be crippling. Don't be surprised if you feel this way, too, especially in the first few hours, days, and weeks following a loss.

Sadness and despair. Loss also provokes feelings of deep sadness, sometimes to the point of despair. If shock and numbness characterize the most common *initial* responses to loss, sadness is the most frequent *longer-term* response. If you were to ask a group of bereaved persons how they felt when their loved one died, most of them would identify sadness as a primary feeling. They might use words like "depressed," "heartbroken," "miserable," "devastated," "hopeless," or something similar to describe their sadness, but they felt sad nonetheless.

Some of us express sadness explicitly, usually through crying or by talking about it. Others of us tend to hold back from expressing sadness, such that those around us remain unaware of how we feel. It could be that we hide our feelings because of discomfort with expressing them. We may feel uneasy with sadness because we have been taught that feeling sad is unacceptable. As a result, we may not accept our sadness. Instead, we push it out of awareness and deny its existence. When intense sadness goes unexpressed, often it turns into despair. We feel hopeless, dejected, and see no light at the end of the dark tunnel of grief. When this hopelessness lasts for an extended period, it tends to become destructive.

Anger, frustration, and impatience. Sometimes we express sadness in the form of anger or frustration. We feel agitated and impatient, and perhaps we lash out at people around us for reasons we may not even understand. Our anger may be just that, true anger, and not an expression of a more fundamental sadness. We may feel furious about our losses. Whether aimed at ourself, a family member, a physician who provided care for a loved one, the deceased person, God, or something else, a deep-seated anger may be our principal response to the loss incurred.

Often anger, frustration, impatience, or related feelings have their basis in a more fundamental experience of sadness. If you find yourself feeling angry in grief, consider trying to explore the basis of that anger. Is this anger an expression of a sadness that you find difficult to express? If so, then what lies behind your responding in an angry manner? Some of us accept and tolerate anger, frustration, or impatience more readily than we do feeling sad or despairing. Does this describe you and your experience? In considering these questions, remember that we benefit from knowing about the potential link between feelings of anger and sadness as we ponder our experiences of loss.

Anxiety, fear, loneliness, vulnerability, and helplessness. Loss may also stir some or all these feelings. You may have any one of these feelings, but fear and anxiety often join with feelings of loneliness, vulnerability, and helplessness.

Most people feel lonely after a significant loss, especially the loss of a person with whom they spent a lot of time. When I served as a pastor, I heard widows and widowers speak frequently of feeling lonely after the spouse died. Several of these people confirmed, in different ways, what one woman said after her husband of fifty-two years died: "The nights are the worst. I dread going to bed because that's when the loneliness becomes almost unbearable." I also listened to those who had lost children, friends, colleagues, and social outlets speak of their loneliness and the pain it caused. We feel lonely because we miss what we once had but have now lost. But sometimes feelings of loneliness are also tied to our fears and anxieties about living with our loss.

I want to point out here that there is a difference between fear and anxiety. Fear has to do with specific, identifiable threats (or perceived threats) to our well-being. You may fear living alone, making financial ends meet, raising children as a single parent, or lacking a sense of purpose without your career. Anxiety is less specific in nature. It relates to feelings of uncertainty, uneasiness, dread, intimidation, worry, or concern, yet it tends to lack an explicit, identifiable object. You may feel anxious about the future, worry about something bad happening, or feel uneasy about moving forward in your grief. It is usually harder to pinpoint what makes us feel anxious than what makes us feel afraid.

Most of us experience a measure of both fear and anxiety following a significant loss. We will identify particular things that make us afraid, but we will also have a wider ranging, if less specific, sense of unease or dread about how to move forward in the absence of what we have lost. Both our fears and our anxieties may link closely with feeling lonely, isolated, vulnerable, or even helpless. When we lose someone or something that provided us with a sense of safety and security in life, we tend to feel unanchored and adrift; we may not know exactly where to turn for refuge.

Physical symptoms. Several physical symptoms can accompany grief. Many people report feeling nauseated or having a churning sensation in the stomach. Others feel empty, especially in their chest and abdomen. People also report experiencing chest pain (a broken heart), a rapid heartbeat, dryness of mouth, difficulty swallowing, feeling short of breath, dizziness, restlessness, sweating, sensitivity to light and noise, chronic and widespread pain, and weakness throughout the body in general. These and other physical sensations are all common in grieving.

Fatigue and exhaustion. Grief often leads to fatigue and even exhaustion. This fatigue affects our physical, emotional, relational, and spiritual states, and may contribute to feeling overwhelmed or depleted. You may find it difficult to get out of bed in the morning. Getting ready for the day or accomplishing routine tasks of daily living also may be a challenge. You may have trouble interacting with others, especially when this requires your emotional as well as physical presence. If these difficulties continue for several weeks following a loss, it is possible that you are experiencing depression. In this case, get in touch with your primary care physician, a counselor or therapist, a psychiatrist, or your minister for assistance. Any of these people should be equipped for helping you discern whether your fatigue may be related to depression, in which case additional professional help is invaluable.

Along with physical exhaustion, grief can also drain us emotionally. Emotional exhaustion often takes the form of feeling detached, disengaged from relationships and life, or lacking feeling altogether. Any of these responses may also indicate depression, and you should consider this possibility. But remember that emotional exhaustion is a normal part of enduring a loss, particularly for the first several weeks.

Loss can also result in spiritual exhaustion. This takes the form of lacking adequate energy to pray, get oneself to church, or maintain a previous level of interest and involvement in religious or spiritual life. Spiritual exhaustion may also bring about difficulty trusting in God's presence, interest, and action in our lives. These spiritual struggles are not unusual.

We need to look no farther than to the Bible to see the common and long-standing link between loss and spiritual fatigue. The Scriptures are filled with cries and petitions offered to God by spiritually and otherwise exhausted persons. One thinks of such examples as: "I am weary with my moaning; every night I flood my bed with tears; I drench my couch with my weeping. My eyes waste away because of grief" (Ps. 6:6–7a); "My eye has grown dim from grief, and all my members are like a shadow" (Job 17:7); and "My life is spent with sorrow, and my years with sighing; my strength fails because of my misery, and my bones waste away" (Ps. 31:10).

Most grief experiences feel exhausting because they call upon us to expend energy that we don't have. Experiencing fear or anxiety in grief, especially when these lead to feeling lonely, vulnerable, or helpless, tends to drain us of our strength and reserves even more.

Regret, guilt, and shame. Many losses involve some measure of regret. Realizing that life will never be the same again is enough to make us feel regretful. We will no longer enjoy a relationship with what we have lost, at least not in the same way, and we wish that we could. We may use words like "disappointment" or "sorrow" to describe our sense of regret.

At times, regret involves something more specific. It may relate to not having said "good-bye" to a loved one who died, or not being present with someone at the time of death. Regret could center on dissatisfaction over some aspect of our relationship, or perhaps another's relationship, to what has been lost. People indicate this kind of regret when they say things like: "I wish I could go back and change some things in our relationship" or "If only he were here, I could explain myself" or "If I had known then what I know now, things could have been very different." Each of these statements points to sorrow over loss, but also to remorse over the inability to change something about a relationship with what has been lost.

More severe and lasting regrets sometimes surface. When this happens, we may consider a loss in terms of feeling guilty and ashamed. Feeling guilty usually involves regret over particular actions or inaction. We feel guilty over something we did or neglected to do as it relates to our loss. Shame, on the other hand, typically has less to do with regret over specific things we have done or not done, and more to do with remorse over *who we have been, or failed to be*, in relation to our loss. We might simplify this distinction by saying that guilt concerns what we have done (or not done) while shame concerns who we are—our very self.

Recall the previous example of regret tied to a lost job. Someone might regret neglecting responsibilities at work, or having injured, mistreated, or disappointed colleagues. Any of these regrets could rise to the level of guilt and shame. Regret might also be tied to a loved one's death. Perhaps we regret spending too little time with her or not communicating our love for her. Maybe we regret dishonesty with her over a significant matter in our life. Perhaps we said hurtful things that we wish we could take back. Possibly we acted in ways that embarrassed this loved one. We now wish not only that we had refrained from such actions, but also that we had made amends before our loved one died. In this case, we might describe our regret as feeling guilty or ashamed, or both.

As you reflect on your own sense of regret surrounding a loss, you will most likely benefit from considering whether and how it links with feeling guilty or ashamed. Many losses cause us to feel regretful, whether associated with a physical death or not. You should not be surprised if you feel regretful, guilty, or ashamed as you grieve. Many people feel this way.

Ambivalence, apathy, satisfaction, and relief. Feeling ambivalent, apathetic, satisfied, or relieved marks some grief experiences. If you feel any of these, you may be surprised and concerned. You may feel guilty or ashamed that you don't have stronger feelings in the wake of your loss (apathy). Or you may struggle with having at least "two minds" when considering your loss (ambivalence). For instance, you might feel both sorrow and joy or satisfaction.

Frances had cared for her ailing husband, Tony, for nearly a decade before he died of complications from Parkinson's disease. During that time, Tony required more and more care. Eventually, Frances could not provide adequate care for Tony by herself, and he was placed in a nursing home. Still, Frances visited Tony every day, for several hours a day. She was devoted to him and loved him very much. When Tony died, Frances shared with me how ashamed she felt because she was "relieved that it was over." She said, "It's hard to admit this, because it feels selfish, but I'm just glad it's over. I miss Tony so much, and it was just awful to watch him decline over the years. But I also feel free now. A huge burden has been lifted, and you know what, that feels great. I want Tony back, but not in the same condition. It was almost too much to bear in the end." Frances felt relieved, but she also felt ashamed that she was "glad that all of this is over." I have known many persons who said that they felt like this.

If you feel any sense of relief or satisfaction after your loss, you may, like Frances, feel ashamed and wonder how you could be so selfish. Such a mixture of feelings can be disconcerting. But before you inflict more pain on yourself, remember that these feelings, though perhaps not what you want, are actually quite common.

Most of us anticipate feeling sad, angry, exhausted, anxious, or afraid, and maybe guilty or ashamed, following a significant loss. We identify these as ordinary responses that flow naturally from losses. But this characterization of grief does not tell the whole story. Many people report having mixed feelings, negative *and* positive, after a loss. They feel some sense of sadness and emptiness. They may even long for what they no longer have in their lives. Yet they also may feel relieved that a burden has been lifted. This relief usually centers on two matters, especially in cases of loss due to the death of a loved one.

First, we may feel relieved that a loved one's suffering has ended. When caring long-term for a chronically ill loved one, we may feel released from a burden when this person dies. After watching a once-strong person deteriorate over time to become a shadow of the former self, we feel a deep sense of relief because this person no longer suffers and is at peace.

Second, we may feel relieved that our own suffering has ended. We no longer have to watch a loved one decline. And we no longer have to provide for her care. Keep in mind that when much of daily life centers on providing care for a chronically or terminally ill person, caregivers get exhausted. We call this common phenomenon "caregiver fatigue." All of us have a limited store of energy, patience, and tolerance in the midst of stressful or painful situations. Eventually, we run out of gas. After a loved one dies, we may feel relieved that we need no longer "run on empty." It is not wrong to feel this way. The one you loved and cared for would be relieved for you as well.

A greater sense of connection, appreciation, and yearning. Another cluster of grief-related feelings includes an increased sense of connection to, and appreciation and yearning for, what has been lost than existed before the loss occurred. As the saying goes, "Absence makes the heart grow fonder." Sometimes we feel less appreciation and desire for what we have when we have it than we feel after we lose it.

For some people, the loss of someone or something they love results in loving the person or thing more than ever before. A surviving spouse may speak of her deceased husband as if he were a saint, longing for him after his death. But when he was alive the couple had a less than perfect relationship in which he behaved in not-always-saintly ways. A person who complained about living in a particular city moves away and begins to talk about that city as if it were paradise. He now longs to return there to live. After being fired from a job, a person begins to hold it in the highest regard and hopes to be rehired. But she may have found little joy or contentment in her job previously, and looked upon it as merely a means to provide a living for her family. Many people who suffer losses experience something similar to these scenarios. Absence does sometimes make the heart grow fonder.

These newfound connections to what we have lost *may* provide comfort. On the one hand, stronger bonds after a loss may ease the pain of absence. Deep connections serve to keep what we love and value close. On the other hand, deeper connections to what we lose can *increase* the pain of grief. Feelings of regret, guilt, or shame may surface as we consider what our relationship with what we have lost could have been or should have been, particularly now that we value it so much more. A deeper appreciation may result in a yearning for what we have lost, and this yearning deepens our pain.

Consider how you feel as you grieve your loss. Try to identify your feelings and accept them as they come. There is nothing wrong with feeling how you feel. Feelings are just feelings, nothing more or less. A wise mentor once encouraged me to remember that feelings are neither good nor bad. We have the tendency to characterize feelings as good or bad, desirable or undesirable, faithful or unfaithful. But this is a mistake. Feelings always have value *as* feelings, whatever their content.

What you *do* with your feelings, however, will not be value neutral. You may deal with them in positive or negative ways. You can act constructively or destructively in light of how you feel. Nevertheless, you should permit yourself to feel what you feel. Only then can you work with your feelings toward constructive ends. So, consider *your* feelings right now. Knowing more about how you feel, and how this relates to your relationship to what you have lost, will contribute to good mourning.

3

What Effect Does Loss Have on How We Think and Behave?

Loss affects not only how we feel but also how we think and behave. So after a loss, it is important to pay close attention to your thoughts and behavior. Notice how both play out and also how they may have changed in light of your loss.

WHAT ARE YOU THINKING?

As you continue to clarify your feelings and seek good mourning, ask yourself this question: What am I thinking? You may also ask *how* you are thinking. Loss affects what we think and how we go about thinking. Loss usually impedes our ability to think clearly, rationally, and critically, especially for the first few days and weeks. But loss can also shape thinking long-term.

Loss can affect thinking about life's value, meaning, and goals. You hear people describe a loss in terms of how it altered their perspective on what truly matters and what they want in life. Loss also affects thinking about current relationships, and relationships that we long for as well. For example, when a family member dies, this can result in renewed relationships with surviving relatives. If a parent dies, we may find ourselves wanting a closer relationship with a surviving sibling more than ever before. At the same time, our losses can influence who we understand ourselves to be and what we're supposed to do with our lives. I know a man, Greg, who decided to change careers after his father died, in order to become a lawyer like his father. Greg had resisted this change for several years, but decided that now he "felt that it was the right time to make it." Someone else, Raul, once told me how strange it felt when both of his parents died: "Life is never the same," he said. "You feel like an orphan." Raul's comment and Greg's career change point out that the loss of those that we love cuts to the core of our self-understanding.

Losses also shape beliefs about God, religious faith, our sense of the cosmos, and the roles that any of these play in our lives. Sometimes losses draw us closer to God, deepen our faith, or motivate us to serve God in new ways. I know people whose faith became more central to their lives after sustaining a painful loss. This was indicated by their devotion to the faith community and its ministries, and also by their commitment to living with greater focus on faith and spiritual matters. Losses also may prompt more reliance upon God and God's provision. This reliance could be tied to hope for a reunion in heaven with what we have lost, or to some other belief concerning the fruit of faith. On other occasions, losses may complicate faith, distance us from God, or make us question former devotions and understandings of life.

Whether having to do with our thinking about God or something else, how we experience a loss influences what we require in order to get through it. This means that when we sustain a loss, how and what we think matters. Both affect how we grieve. As you clarify your own thoughts, consider the ways that loss can affect thinking, described below.

Common Ways That Loss Affects Thinking

Grief can bring about states of disbelief, denial, or mistrust; disorientation, disorganization, or confusion; identification or association; preoccupation or obsession; and denial or disregard. Let's consider each of these states.

Disbelief, denial, or mistrust. Just as shock and numbness are the most common initial grief-related *feelings*, disbelief tends to be the most common initial state of thinking. When we learn of a significant loss, most of us will simply not believe it. At first, losses seem unreal. We cannot tolerate them. They fall within the realm of a bad dream that we find difficult, if not impossible, to accept as true. Sudden or unforeseen losses usually result in a more pronounced and prolonged state of disbelief. Having no time to anticipate or prepare for a loss makes believing it all the more challenging.

But almost any loss will take us somewhat by surprise. Even if we have anticipated a loss, we can never fully prepare for its impact. So you should not be alarmed if you find yourself thinking or saying, "I just can't believe this is happening," "I keep thinking that I'm going to see him pull into the driveway after work, just as he always did," "I cannot accept that I got passed over for this promotion," or "I refuse to believe this." These statements point to the difficulty that most people have with believing that a loss has transpired, especially when they first receive the news.

Remember that an initial state of disbelief, and even denial, serves a protective function. The mind recognizes that information it has received will be heartbreaking. So at first we disbelieve it. In time, we will consider believing it. But this happens on our own terms. The need to receive and manage painful news at our own pace is why most of us mistrust the news at first. We tend to respond to losses with an initial state of skepticism, if not denial, because we need to manage the pain that comes with loss. After a few days, we usually will begin to believe what has occurred. But we may also dip back into a state of disbelief or denial, perhaps repeatedly. This can happen for several weeks or longer. Moving back and forth between states of believing and disbelieving helps marshal coping resources to prepare for grief's sting.

Our state of preparedness relates to several factors. One is the nature of our loss, including what we lost, how we lost it, and the suddenness with which it occurred. Losses that we anticipate to some degree, though painful, tend to be coped with better than sudden losses that take us by surprise. For most people, it is easier to handle a loved one's death caused by cancer than death from a sudden heart attack or a suicide. Losses that we can see coming usually allow us to say "good-bye" or otherwise prepare ourselves for the pain of loss. Although we are never fully prepared, anticipating a loss can help lessen its pain. Sudden deaths provide no time to prepare. This is why they tend to hit us with more force and inflict more pain. Other factors that relate to our preparedness for loss include the strength of our attachments and our means for coping as we grieve.

These means for coping come from within us (internal means) and also from beyond us (external means). Internal means have to do with personal disposition, temperament, and what we might call "inner fortitude." These include our inclination for hope, our ability to solve problems and communicate effectively, and our resilience. Ability for self-awareness, self-confidence, and trust also informs internal means for coping. So does almost any personal trait that helps to sustain a sense of safety, security, meaning, and identity when these come under threat.

External means for coping include our reliance upon family members, friends, neighbors, colleagues, and the faith community. Of course, our relationship to God provides needed sustenance for many of us. So do ministers, counselors, therapists, or spiritual directors. Think about how you may draw from as many of these means for coping as possible. Look within yourself for support. Look to those around you, too. Look also to God to sustain you as you grieve.

A principal means for coping with loss, then, involves the back-and-forth movement between belief and denial. But if, after a couple of weeks, you find that you spend more time denying your loss than recognizing its actuality, pay attention to this. You may need more support from your minister, spiritual director, a professional counselor, or someone else with expertise on bereavement-related concerns. Within a few days after your loss, it will be important for you to consider your ability to believe that you have experienced a great loss. Believing is essential for beginning the journey of getting through it.

Disorientation, disorganization, or confusion. Loss usually prevents us from thinking clearly. Even after an initial state of disbelief has passed, we still may find it difficult to maintain focus in our thinking. Concentrating on particular responsibilities or operations may prove especially challenging. Whether at work or leisure, we may check out at times and have difficulty staying on task.

Difficulty with short-term memory may also occur. Loss can disorient us so much that we struggle to remember things. You may find it difficult to remember matters associated with the event of the loss itself. Or you may struggle to recall other things in its aftermath. Examples include difficulty remembering details in conversations you have, recalling a sequence of events you were a part of, or putting together various facts or figures that you ordinarily would find easy.

Loss affects memory because it curbs the ability to concentrate. Without concentration, our experiences don't register in memory as they otherwise would. So you may find yourself asking people to remind you of something you cannot recall. You may have to ask someone to repeat what she told you a few minutes earlier. You may have to request that someone go over details or a sequence of events in a story that you have heard several times before.

You'll want to keep in mind that other aspects of grief come into play here, too. These may further affect your ability to think clearly. Conditions like fatigue, anger, deep-seated regret, and especially anxiety or fear usually challenge the ability to focus, concentrate, and organize thoughts. So don't be surprised, or distressed, if you experience disorientation, disorganization, or confusion in your thinking. You may expect this in the first moments following a loss, but it may continue for several weeks later and perhaps even longer.

Identification, association, preoccupation, or obsession. Another cluster of thinking-related grief responses bears mention. Significant loss sometimes triggers stronger identification or association with what we have lost than we ever experienced before. Earlier I mentioned how loss can strengthen feelings of connection to, and appreciation and yearning for, what we have lost. Loss may also have a similar effect on our thinking.

After a parent dies, for example, we may think about what this parent would have wanted for us in situations that we face. We might concern ourselves with how "Mom" would have responded or how she would want us to respond. We could find ourselves operating with assumptions that bear a striking resemblance to those of our deceased parent, whereas before this parent's death we held different assumptions and would have responded in a different manner.

These occasions for identification and association usually relate to our desire to maintain a close connection to what we have lost. Typically we are unaware of this new degree of identification, yet we nonetheless take on various qualities of what has been lost. These qualities permeate our selves and lives as never before. Feeling more connected to what we have lost, we maintain its presence in our lives.

In extreme forms, though, identification or association can turn to preoccupation or obsession. When this happens, our lives are governed more by what we have lost than by our capacity for making decisions ourselves. When the identification is with a deceased person, what we perceive to be her desires for us trump our own desires. You can expect to experience some of this identification and association in your thinking after a loss. But if you feel that you are beginning to allow the other person to take over your life, to govern it from the grave, you should share this with a minister, counselor, or other helping professional.

HOW ARE YOU BEHAVING?

As you clarify your feelings and thoughts and seek good mourning, another question to ask is, How am I behaving? If a loss affects how you feel and think, it also affects your conduct. It influences how you interact with other people. It affects how social or isolated you become. It also affects your energy level and desire for various types of activity, whether physical, mental, or spiritual. Sometimes, loss brings about avoidant or destructive behaviors. Pay attention to how you behave as you grieve. Clarity about this may also help you know more about how you are feeling and thinking as you grieve. This is because how we behave relates closely to how we feel and think.

Common Ways That Loss Affects Behavior

Think of grief-related behaviors as falling under three broad headings. These are *sociability*, *avoidance/seeking behavior*, and *destructive/ constructive behavior*. Let's consider each of these. As we do so, think about how any of these clusters of behaviors relate to how *you* are behaving in your grief.

Sociability. Loss impacts relationships. Positively, losses can prompt a greater investment of time and energy with those most significant to us. After a loss we may treasure loved ones and the relationships that we share with them more than ever before. As a result, we may seek the presence of significant others frequently, doing all that we can to shore up these relationships. We assume that we will gain comfort and support from these relationships. This eases the pain of loss and helps sustain us as we grieve.

On the negative side, loss can strain relationships. Sustaining a loss may lead to difficulty communicating with family members, friends, or coworkers. Loss may result in trouble getting along with them, leading to more disagreement or arguing than ever before. Loss may trigger anger, frustration, or irritation that is self-directed, aimed at other persons, or both.

Sometimes loss involves withdrawal from significant relationships. We isolate ourselves emotionally and physically, becoming less social and available to our close associates. We also may disengage from work or work-related functions. Another type of withdrawal occurs when we devote less attention, time, or energy to hobbies or other passions. Pay attention to whether your "sociability" has changed since your loss. If it has, try to discern to what extent it has changed and the particular ways it has changed. For most of us, maintaining significant relationships *and* drawing strength from them remain essential for getting through our losses.

Avoidance/seeking behaviors. Surrounding ourselves with other people can also be a way to avoid thinking about a loss. We may attempt to avoid the pain of grief by finding ways not to be alone, when losses tend to be most on our minds. Do you seek the presence of others in uncharacteristic ways as a means for not having to be by yourself and thus to escape awareness of your pain?

We also may try to stay so busy that we lack both the time and psychological space to think about what has occurred. Might people be saying things like this about you? "Joe is just not himself these days. He's so hard to talk to; he won't stop long enough." "Lucy is busier than ever before, she's always on the run." Or do you find yourself being kept so busy by people's well-intentioned efforts that you often think, "I just need to be alone"?

We may also attempt to avoid the pain of grief by removing ourselves from reminders of what we have lost. This type of avoidance may be behind our purging our home or office of pictures, clothing, mementos, or other keepsakes associated with our loss.[1] Avoidance occurs, too, when we will not speak of our loss or when we forbid others to speak of it in our presence. Think about whether your loss has brought avoidant or seeking behaviors. If it has, and if this continues for several weeks, you may benefit from talking to your minister, counselor, or another helping person.

Destructive or constructive behaviors. Sometimes loss generates destructive behaviors, particularly when the loss involves feelings of anger, regret, or anxiety. You may find yourself overeating, abusing drugs or alcohol, avoiding exercise, or otherwise neglecting your health. Some bereaved persons become careless behind the wheel of an automobile, engage in irresponsible sexual behaviors, or otherwise assume a devil-may-care attitude that leads to dangerous behavior. This attitude and its behaviors usually relate to one of two things. The pain is so severe that we opt for some form of self-harm to end the pain. Or we may feel that nothing really matters now that this loss has occurred, and therefore opt to "throw caution to the wind." Younger persons seem to respond to loss in this way more often than older ones. But there is the potential for destructive behavior in grief in all of us. If destructive behavior begins, you need to recognize it and seek professional help immediately. The stakes may be too high to delay.

Losses can also lead to constructive behaviors. Loss may lead us to pay more attention to our health and lifestyle. I know a woman who had been obese for most of her life. After her husband died at a young age, she began to take better care of her health. She lost a significant amount of weight, began to eat well, and started an exercise regimen that she continues to maintain. A loss may also trigger greater appreciation for the persons, places, and things that we enjoy in life. And loss can inspire us to deeper commitment to the norms and values of our faith tradition. Sometimes loss results in a new or renewed devotion to serving others.

My friend David Lee Jones suggests a practice worth considering. When someone significant to him dies, he identifies an admirable quality or passion in that person's life. He then seeks to incorporate it in his own life. David tells the story of how he took part several years ago in the funeral service of a colleague who was passionate about the environment. This was at a time when focusing on the environment was less common than it is today. On the way home from the funeral, David stopped at a local hardware store and purchased bins to use for recycling. He began this practice of recycling because he wanted something constructive to flow from his painful experience of loss.

There are many other ways that loss can result in positive changes in our lives. Although loss may bring devastating pain, this pain need not prove destructive. It may serve as a source for improving your own life and the lives of others. Why not begin thinking about how you are behaving, and especially about how you might use your pain for something constructive.

In the next chapter, I suggest ways to cope with loss, to manage feelings, thoughts, and behaviors. As we proceed, remember the distinction between grief and mourning. Grief describes how we respond to loss, including our feelings, thoughts, and behaviors. Enhancing our awareness and understanding of these responses, and coping well with them, prepare us to mourn in healthy, whole, and faithful ways. Mourning describes how we go about getting through and beyond our loss and come to value living again. As I suggest strategies for coping with loss in the next chapter, keep in mind that you need to grieve before you mourn.

4

What Helps Us Cope with Loss?

Loss causes pain because it threatens our sense of safety, security, meaning, identity, and pleasure. This pain raises the question of what we need to do when we suffer the loss of someone or something that we love. The short answer is this: We need to mourn. In part 2 I suggest ways for engaging the mourning process in order to move through the pain of loss. First, though, in this concluding chapter of part 1, let's consider ways to prepare for mourning.

The best preparation for mourning is to cope well with the many responses involved in grief. Coping well in your grief sets the stage for mourning. Consider the following strategies for coping with your feelings, thoughts, and behaviors as you grieve your loss. These can be utilized in any order, and according to what you think will be most helpful.

STRATEGIES FOR COPING WITH YOUR LOSS

Rehearse the events associated with learning about your loss in as much detail as you can tolerate. Try to recall where you were when you received the devastating news. Recollect the words used by the person who shared it. Repeat them several times as a way to take yourself back to that point in time where life as you knew it was forever changed. This advice may seem strange, if not downright cruel. Why would we subject ourselves repeatedly to something so painful by rehearsing its details? But reflecting on our experience in this way actually has tremendous value. We usually need to "wake up" from a state of being numbed by loss. A good way to awaken ourselves is to rehearse the events surrounding our loss in as much detail as possible. Seeing the word "rehearse" in the context of our discussion may prompt thoughts of a "hearse," a vehicle used for transporting caskets. But this is a relatively new meaning. The Latin word from which we get *hearse* originally meant "harrow." A harrow was an instrument used in agriculture. It consisted of metal teeth used to turn and break apart dirt that had already been plowed. Harrowing cultivated the soil. It activated nutrients, "awakening" the soil in preparation for future planting.[1]

So think of "rehearsing" how you first learned of your loss as a way to help cultivate the soil of mourning. In order to mourn, you first need to awaken to the reality of your loss and cope with the various feelings, thoughts, and behaviors it brings. "Turning over" and "breaking apart" the circumstances of learning about the loss can foster this awakening and coping. Like harrowing soil to prepare for future planting, rehearsing the events associated with how you learned about your loss prepares you for a future marked by good mourning.

Your rehearsal may occur in conversation with other persons. You may benefit from the support that a trusted friend, family member, pastor, or helping professional provides. Or you may choose to "rehearse" in dialogue with yourself. Either, or both, may prove beneficial for grieving. Furthermore, it may be several days, or even a couple of weeks, before you feel ready to do this—or, as ready as you will ever feel to do it. Nevertheless, it needs to happen and, for most people, the sooner the better. The need to rehearse the details of your loss will likely diminish with time and as you attend to grieving.

Place yourself in the presence of reminders of what you have lost. When we feel ready to do so, we benefit from pushing ourselves to encounter the pain and absence of loss. Interacting with reminders of our loss provides for these encounters. We interact with our loss when visiting a grave site or looking at pictures of a loved one who has died. We also interact with our loss when holding mementos from a marriage or other significant romantic relationship that has ended, viewing a résumé or something else tied to a lost job, or reading diary or journal entries recounting a dream that has gone unfulfilled. Interacting with reminders of what we have lost is painful, and sometimes excruciating. Therefore, we need to tread carefully when approaching these reminders. Remember, though, that this kind of interaction usually proves helpful for grieving. In time, as you move through grief and begin to mourn, you probably will not need to take up these reminders of what you have lost as frequently. For the first few weeks, however, and perhaps longer, reminders of what you have lost may prove indispensable for helping you grieve.

Recognize the value of funerals, and participate in them. In losses due to death, the funeral may offer what we need most, at least initially, for coping with loss. People who don't think of themselves as "religious" sometimes opt not to have a funeral for a loved one. Nor might they want one for themselves. But even if we bracket for a moment the theological or religious reasons for funerals, there are still several good reasons to consider having them.

First, funerals put us in the presence of the body or ashes of the deceased, particularly when the funeral includes a "viewing" or "wake." Although some will find it difficult to view a dead loved one's body, you are strongly encouraged to do so. Seeing a loved one dead, though usually painful, makes the loss more real. Confronting its reality, literally face-to-face, fosters "owning" the loss and its effects. People confirm this when they say things like "I couldn't believe that he was gone until I saw him there in the casket" or "It wasn't until we put her in the ground that it hit me: I'm never going to see her again." Such statements indicate the powerful effect of seeing a loved one's dead body or watching the burial. Thomas Lynch, a professional funeral director who writes about experiences of death and loss, suggests that a funeral without a body is like a wedding without a bride! As brides make weddings meaningful and memorable for those who attend, dead bodies do the same for funerals.

Second, funerals present opportunities for family members and close associates to experience a loss together. Common experience also helps make a loss more real and promotes coping with it in a straightforward manner. Sometimes funeral gatherings include opportunities to speak directly about the deceased person's life and legacy. This practice may continue well beyond the funeral too. Talking about a person's life, especially in the past tense, usually proves beneficial for those who grieve. It proves beneficial because it helps to confirm that a loved one has in fact died. We need this confirmation as we experience the normal process of moving back and forth between acknowledging a loss and denying it.

Similarly, most funerals include time for sharing personal feelings about the loss of someone loved. Sometimes we share our feelings more formally, as in the context of a religious service. When I was serving a congregation as its pastor, I would include a time for family and friends to share their feelings and experiences during the funeral. But sometimes we feel more comfortable sharing our feelings about loss more privately, perhaps in conversation with another person at the funeral home. Either way, talking about the life of one who has died and, just as important, sharing how we are faring with our own loss promote coping with what we have lost. Reflecting on what we have lost and on how we are faring brings us face-to-face with loss and encourages its reception head-on.

So I think we should consider resisting the urge to engage exclusively in small talk at funerals. Instead, it is important to speak about the person who has died. You might speak also about how you feel about this loss and how it impacts your life. As you do so, it's good to invite others to do the same. A shared experience of this type can promote solidarity in loss that provides its own comfort and encouragement. It's often helpful to keep on talking about your experience of loss for some time following the funeral.

One potential problem with funerals is that in most religious traditions they occur very soon after a loss. Some faith traditions base this practice on central theological beliefs. And practical ends may be served by attending to the burial or cremation expeditiously. In most cases, it's impractical if not impossible to delay burial, although in cold weather climates where the ground is frozen in winter months, such delay is not unusual. Nevertheless, although having a funeral so soon after a loss may offer certain comforts, it can also pose difficulties for grief and mourning. Consider that most funerals take place between one and four days following death. Most people are still in states of shock and disbelief during this period. These states reduce some of the potential benefits that funerals present to those who have suffered a loss. I have mentioned how helpful it can be for the grieving to see the body of a deceased loved one. Funerals provide an opportunity for this encounter. But during the first few days after a loved one's death, most of us don't possess the emotional (feeling) or cognitive (thinking) space required for fully taking in the funeral experience and its other benefits. For this reason, funerals might offer more lasting aids for grief and mourning if they were to take place a few weeks after death occurs.

One way to prolong the benefits of a funeral is to videotape it for viewing later. This is common practice for weddings. Couples and families have a video record of a most significant life event. They may revisit that event whenever and as often as they want, taking from it new experiences and insights. The same practice may offer potential benefits with regard to funerals. Having the opportunity to revisit such a significant life event, especially after the shock, disorientation, and the most acute pain of grief has begun to wane, may provide lasting benefits for mourning. For example, you may listen again to the pastor's sermon, the prayers and music offered, or the reflections of family members and other loved ones. Any of this may be meaningful and comforting.

Many people who read this book will likely read it after a loved one's funeral has taken place. When this is the case, you may want to think about similar rituals that you can take part in at a later date. Some possibilities are mentioned below. Also, keep the benefits of funerals in mind when you experience future losses. Funerals may help you mourn well.

Remind yourself that your feelings are natural and acceptable. Sometimes we increase the pain of loss by deeming our feelings unwarranted, insignificant, selfish, or otherwise inappropriate. We say things like "I shouldn't feel this way," "I'm acting childish by being angry," "This is so self-indulgent," or "Enough—I need to move on and put this behind me." In thinking this way, you fail to recognize that "putting this behind me" almost always requires first accepting how you feel and affirming its legitimacy.

Remember that feelings are neither good nor bad in themselves. What we do with our feelings can become positive or negative, for we may work out our feelings in either constructive or destructive ways. But in themselves, feelings are *just feelings*. We have to risk allowing ourselves to feel however we feel and to accept this as OK. Only then can we begin to work with our feelings toward constructive, positive, faithful, and other desirable ends.

Part of acceptance may involve recognizing that feelings may be "both/and," not just "either/or." Seemingly contrasting or opposite feelings are not always mutually exclusive. You may feel sad and relieved, guilty and ambivalent, fatigued and eager to move on with your life, all at the same time. Your feelings will likely vacillate and seem contradictory. We expect this to occur when grieving a loss.

Sometimes just reminding ourselves that what we feel is OK, natural, and expected proves helpful. Having others remind us of this can also be beneficial. Whatever our feelings following a loss, assurance that what we experience is more or less normal and acceptable tends to grant a measure of relief. With this in mind, it may help you to remind yourself that what you feel is OK. You may also benefit from finding someone, or a couple of people, who will remind you of this as well.

Express yourself. Expressing feelings decreases the power that they hold over us and provides a sense of relief. Failing to express feelings carries a particularly destructive potential—emotionally, relationally, physically, and spiritually. When we articulate our pain, we externalize it. Metaphorically speaking, we remove it from our interior life. We place it outside ourselves. As a result, we have the ability to examine our pain, understand it, and interact with it in new ways. All of this usually serves to reduce pain's power over us. Why? Because we face it head-on. We dare to examine it closely, face-to-face. We seek to understand it better. In doing these things we have a better chance of coping with pain and its effects.

Unvoiced emotions, however, have a tendency to strengthen and become destructive. As we try to keep these emotions inside, or push them out of our awareness, they take on a life of their own. Unexpressed feelings of anger and frustration tend to become most destructive.

If you feel angry or frustrated, think about sharing your feelings with those who are the objects of your anger or frustration. This has several potential benefits. First, "getting it off your chest" may reduce your anger and frustration so that neither you nor your relationships continue to suffer the ill effects. Second, sharing your anger, disappointment, frustration, or similar feelings may help move you toward a state of forgiveness and, eventually, reconciliation with parties that have offended you. When anger or resentment is a primary emotion, you eventually need to forgive and seek reconciliation if you are to experience good mourning. Forgiveness and reconciliation remain ends in themselves, of course. These are central to an emotionally healthy and faithful life. But forgiveness and reconciliation also pave the way for mourning well. Both require expressing your feelings to those who have offended you.

If you choose not to express your feelings to offending parties, you may express them to someone else. I am not advocating gossip or speaking out of turn. But it may prove helpful to share feelings with a trusted friend or confidant, if you don't share them with the one who has offended you. One of life's great blessings is having someone with whom we can share feelings, and who will allow us simply to feel as we do and to express these feelings as we have the need.

You may also choose to express yourself through artistic means, such as painting, writing poetry, playing music, or keeping a journal that only you see. Artistic expression can certainly join with other types of expression mentioned. In fact, you will do well to think about expressing yourself in multiple ways. However you decide to express yourself, commit to doing so. It's worth it.

Talk about your experience with a friend, a family member, or both. A primary way for expressing ourselves is through extended conversations with others. Most of us will find few things more helpful than this in our grief and mourning. As Shakespeare urged in *Macbeth*, "Give sorrow words; the grief that does not speak / Whispers the oe'r-fraught heart and bids it break."[2]

We cannot put all of our experience into words. There will always be a remainder of experience impossible to conceive, much less voice. Tennyson tells us as much in a poem written after the death of a close friend. There he notes that words "half reveal / and half conceal the Soul within," and that the "large grief which these enfold / Is given in outline and no more."[3] But we benefit from trying our best to give words to experiences of loss and sharing them with someone else. Gaining even an "outline" of our authentic feelings and sharing it on multiple occasions with a trusted friend or confidant holds great potential for healing and wholeness.

For reasons we don't completely understand, talking about painful experiences with another person usually helps us feel better. Perhaps this relates to our innate need for relationships. Both Jewish and Christian traditions hold that God created us *not* to live in isolation from others—whether physically, emotionally, or relationally—but for close relationship. We might call this communion. As the biblical account of creation puts it, God declared that "it is not good that the man should be alone; I will make him a helper as his partner" (Gen. 2:18). Sharing our grief and its pain with someone close to us, such as a friend or family member, fosters a kind of communion. This may help ease the hurt that we feel. It also may help relieve the other person's pain, particularly if she is grieving too. Living through a painful experience in communion with another that you value may help ease burdens for both of you.

Talking about loss may prove difficult. Although necessary for grieving and mourning well, engaging reality in this way may be the last thing you feel prepared to do. Nevertheless, you are encouraged to find ways to do it. This does not require formalized talking, as occurs in counseling or therapy, though it could. Simply finding a person to listen to you and encourage you to talk specifically and with as much depth as possible about your loss will foster good mourning.

Talk about your experience with a minister, a counselor, or a spiritual director. As helpful as speaking of your grief with a friend, loved one, or other close associate may be, speaking to a minister, counselor, or spiritual guide may prove even more beneficial. Sometimes we gain the most from speaking with someone who can claim a bit more emotional distance from us and our situation than the typical friend or family member. Furthermore, ministers, counselors, and spiritual directors have training and experience with helping navigate the bereavement journey.

When you feel that you need assistance with what could be termed "spiritual" or "faith-related" concerns, then a minister or spiritual director may be the best option. These persons typically help you identify ways to reestablish hope in the midst of despair by drawing on religious or spiritual wisdom. If you are less inclined to think about your experience in spiritual terms, then a counselor (psychologist, clinical social worker, licensed professional counselor) may be more helpful. They, too, will have training and experience in helping with grief-related matters. Or the best solution may be a relationship with *both* types of helpers. Whatever you decide, tapping the vast resources of a well-trained and experienced clergyperson, pastoral counselor, other professional, or some combination of these, can help you cope with your feelings.

Welcome your tears. Crying serves a healing purpose. When we cry, we release a multitude of emotions and physical burdens associated with our painful experience. This release not only comforts us but also prepares us to move forward in our journey through loss.

The Scriptures advise us to cry when we hurt. As the author of Lamentations urges, "Cry aloud to the Lord! O wall of daughter Zion! Let tears stream down like a torrent day and night! Give yourself no rest, your eyes no respite!" (Lam. 2:18). The Scriptures also offer assurance that God sees our tears (2 Kgs. 20:5; Isa. 38:5) and speak of a future when God wipes away all tears of sorrow (Isa. 25:8; Rev. 7:17; 21:4). Reminiscent of Jesus' words in the Sermon on the Mount, God's presence and love abide, sustaining us through every time of pain. Never do the Scriptures devalue tears. They assure us, however, that our tears will not have the last word.

Some of us will be more prone to crying than others. Someone I know for whom crying comes rather easily describes herself as a faucet. For others, crying proves more difficult. The faucet may be stopped up. Maybe it has never been tapped in the first place. Those for whom crying proves more difficult may have a sense that crying indicates weakness, immaturity, or a lack of self-control. They feel embarrassed about the prospect of shedding tears. You'll hear them say things like "I don't want to get emotional at the funeral" or "I'm afraid I'll 'lose it' if I go to the cemetery." These comments indicate that expressing emotions feels unacceptable.

Perhaps you feel this way yourself. But rather than resist crying, remember that we usually benefit from allowing ourselves to "get emotional" and even "lose it" for the sake of feeling relieved and, eventually, mourning well. The ancient poet and philosopher Seneca, whose stoic approach to life would never have been deemed overly emotional or as lacking control, nevertheless recognized the great value of tears. He urged that we "let tears flow of their own accord: their flowing is not inconsistent with inward peace and harmony." Far from being undesirable, tears often lead to feeling relieved and more at peace. Perhaps you will shed tears alone. Maybe you will shed them in another's presence or arms. Whatever the case, you may welcome your tears and their healing capacity. Remember that Jesus himself was moved to tears upon the death of his close friend Lazarus (John 11:35).

Surround yourself with people, places, and activities that you enjoyed before your loss occurred. One of the best ways to get through intense sadness is recalling what provided joy, excitement, and meaning *before* your loss. In recalling these, you may enlist their help in your current state. These people, places, and activities likely will not become a cure-all for your sadness. Furthermore, you may have lost interest in them as a result of your bereavement, especially activities associated with what you lost. Nevertheless, what once contributed to your happiness and contentment can in some measure do so again. Trying to surround yourself with whatever brought you joy and peace in the past can prove helpful for coping after a loss occurs.

Seek the presence of those who comfort you. When we feel anxious or afraid, relief often comes when we spend time with people who comfort us. Anxiety breeds isolation. This increases feelings of loneliness and helplessness. Of course, when we feel anxious, few things may prove more challenging than being with others. Many people who feel anxious try to manage their anxiety by withdrawing from others, especially if the anxiety links with feelings of embarrassment or shame. Nevertheless, the presence of even one person with whom we may share our struggles, and who offers encouragement and a sense of security, can help sustain us. Many people find comfort and respite simply by being in the presence of the people they love.

Perhaps you will want to talk about your loss with someone who comforts you. Maybe that person will help you reflect on what you have lost, but also to dream about a future when your pain has eased and you find joy in life again. Consider seeking the presence of God through prayer, worship, and other faith practices. This can provide unmatched means of comfort and grace. I will say more about this later in chapters 7 and 8.

Place yourself in physical settings that offer comfort. Many of us find comfort when we go to particular places, take in certain scenery or views, or locate ourselves in settings that we find beautiful or meaningful. For some, the natural world provides a haven. For others, respite comes with spending time in sacred spaces like church sanctuaries or retreat centers. Some people find it restful to locate for a time in a setting that simply differs from the place where they usually spend the bulk of their day. Examples of these places of respite might include the countryside, the woods, lakes, beaches, the mountains, parks, bookstores, coffee houses, art museums, and even a special room or part of our home that invites us to "get away," relax, and rest. Identifying places that comfort you and spending time in them can provide needed respite.

Engage in other activities that offer comfort, rest, and promote recovery. This will probably require reducing responsibilities and commitments as much as possible. It may also call for pampering yourself in ways that you ordinarily would decline. For example, you may allow for an extra hour of sleep each night, or perhaps for taking a nap during the day. Perhaps you will spend more time listening to music, reading a book, taking a shower or bath, or eating favorite foods. It may be that you have energy to meditate or pray for a few minutes. Doing so often helps simultaneously to relax and energize the body and mind.

You may also find respite reading Scriptures or singing hymns. Some people will have the means to get a massage or relax in a whirlpool. Some also find comfort through sexual intimacy with the one they love. A friend recently told me about how he found comfort in sex with his wife after his sister's death from cystic fibrosis at age thirty-seven. This loss hit him very hard. He said, "My wife sensed that I needed extra special love, and she initiated sex frequently for several weeks after Elizabeth's death. It was very healing, very special, and I look back on that time in our marriage as one of the most wonderful times. Her warm, unexpected, wonderful love reminded me of Genesis 24:67, where Rebekah's love comforted Isaac after the death of his mother Sarah." For my friend, sexual intimacy with the one he loved was healing, even sacred.

For some, sexual intimacy may be associated with the one whom one has lost and, therefore, be painful. Maybe another type of intimacy, or something else, will serve them better. Remember, the idea here is simply to make your environment as comfortable as possible, which is conducive to rest, helping conserve energy, and in some cases to providing energy as well.

Engage in moderate exercise and physical activity. Exercising during grief may seem counterintuitive. If we feel exhausted, we usually refrain from exerting ourselves, right? In fact, however, pushing ourselves toward physical activity often results in more energy, not less, and exercise offers numerous physical benefits. Exercise also has positive effects on emotions and the ability to think clearly. Moderate physical activity can contribute to overall well-being when we grieve.

Consider taking a fifteen-to-thirty-minute walk or doing some light stretching exercises each day. If you are accustomed to more regular and intense workouts, think about resuming these activities, even if to a lesser degree. If you are a runner, go for a short run. If you swim, go to the gym, or play tennis regularly, keep with your routine as best you can. If you take daily walks, do your best to continue these. Whatever forms of physical activity you choose, you will benefit from exercising regularly. One way to ensure this is to enlist the help of an exercise partner or buddy who helps you remain consistent and holds you accountable for it, precisely when this proves most difficult.

Remember your errors, but do not allow them to consume you. It usually helps to revisit our regrets. This fosters grieving a loss more authentically and prepares us for mourning. One way to revisit regret involves examining how we have erred or neglected to fulfill our responsibilities. This approach helps identify what we have done, or failed to do, that contributed to our feeling regretful, which may prevent us from making similar mistakes in the future. Another way to address feelings of regret involves apologizing to those whom we have wronged. In other words, we may ask for forgiveness. We may not be able to make reparation entirely. Our efforts may not alter what we have lost. But even so, attempting to right the situation may relieve feelings of regret. This allows us to grieve in more beneficial ways.

We also want to identify other ways to live more authentically in the presence of our loss. This fosters getting through the loss in more beneficial ways. In general, paying close attention to how we feel, what we think, and how we behave serves the goals of authenticity.

Work on forgiving and being reconciled. Jesus speaks about the need for forgiveness and reconciliation. He attends to these matters in the context of the prevailing wisdom provided by Jewish tradition concerning the violence that human beings inflict on one another. He says, "You have heard that it was said to those of ancient times, 'You shall not murder'; and 'whoever murders shall be liable to judgment.' But I say to you that if you are angry with a brother or sister, you will be liable to judgment; and if you insult a brother or sister, you will be liable to the council. . . . So when you are offering your gift at the altar, if you remember that your brother or sister has something against you, leave your gift there before the altar and go; first be reconciled to your brother or sister, and then come and offer your gift" (Matt. 5:21–24).

Jesus confirms here that reconciliation, which requires forgiveness, should receive priority attention. Of more immediate importance than offering our gift to God is seeking reconciliation with those from whom we have become alienated and estranged. Forgiveness and reconciliation don't require that we forget, condone, minimize, or dismiss injustices that we have suffered. Nor should we let go of anger prematurely in an effort to facilitate forgiveness and reconciliation. Anger serves a healthy and even *holy* purpose. It allows us to say, "This is not acceptable" when violence or injustice comes our way. But we need to find ways to express anger, sitting with it appropriately and for a period of time, and then let it go as we live more fully into Jesus' command. As the saying goes, "To err is human, to forgive, divine." More often than not, we need to rely on God to help us forgive, to move us toward a kind of reconciliation that we cannot accomplish alone.

A few years ago, my friend Henry Summerall reflected on the question, "How can we forgive someone who has died?" in a devotional that he wrote for members of his congregation. Henry wrote of his relationship with his deceased father. The two had a good relationship. They enjoyed being together, took some great trips when Henry was growing up, and even "shared some secrets." Henry loved his father deeply. Nevertheless, Henry had been troubled for years by something hurtful that his father said to him. Despite the pain it caused him, Henry never brought it up and his father died before it got resolved.

A few weeks after his death, Henry began having frequent bad dreams. He writes, "The scenes varied, but they always ended up in us having a vicious shouting argument. I knew in my spirit that this unresolved issue was the problem keeping things from being right between us." Henry decided to pray about his need to forgive his father. "In prayer I told God about this situation and told God that I forgive Daddy, in words something like this: 'Dear Lord, in Jesus' name I forgive Daddy for that terrible thing he said to me that has hurt me so badly. Please, you forgive him, too.'" Henry notes that he prayed this only once, and that he soon felt a peace about this matter that had eluded him before. He writes, "God answered my prayer. Several nights later I had another dream about me and Daddy taking a trip, and we were laughing and talking away and having such a great time being together, and there was so much love flowing between us. I knew God had answered my prayer, and that everything was fine between me and Daddy. Those bad dreams have never returned."

Faith can play a central role in helping us through loss. We turn to God *in faith* to help us forgive and make amends with others. This reliance on God and God's promise to provide for our need is called "grace." We live gracefully in relationship to God. God's grace serves as the basis for living gracefully with our neighbors. So it is often helpful to find ways to draw strength and resolve from our faith as we grieve.

This is true especially when loss involves anger or alienation that sep-
arates us from others. Perhaps you need to work on forgiving someone,
and this will help you along your journey through loss.

Focus on the present, not the future. Many people who grieve focus too
much on the future. As a result, they don't attend sufficiently to the
present. Eventually, a future focus will be essential for the mourning
process. At the appropriate time (perhaps after several weeks or, more
likely, months), we need to embrace a future orientation to life in the
wake of a loss. Nevertheless, this focus on the future may prove detri-
mental for someone who has just recently begun to grieve.

Settling into a future focus too quickly tends to work against having
confidence that pain will eventually subside. By looking so intently at
the future, we lose sight of what needs to happen, and what we need to
secure, presently. Losing sight of our present needs, we may not attend
to them. By not attending to them, the pain and challenges of loss may
worsen. As these worsen, we may lose confidence in things becoming
better, not only in the present but also in the future. Think of it like
this. If you constantly peer over the horizon, looking for a better future,
you fail to see what is directly in front of you. Failing to see this, you
neglect to attend to it. Therefore, your situation gets worse, not better, and this adds to your pain, feelings of helplessness, and lack of hope.
Intensely painful experiences regularly carry with them a sense that life
will never be good again.

So rather than casting too quick a gaze toward the future and missing the opportunity to take care of what you need now, simply look
at what today brings and requires. You may remind yourself of the
wisdom provided by an ancient Chinese proverb, namely, that a ten-
thousand-mile journey begins with the first step. Instead of presuming
that you need to figure out immediately how to travel the longer journey through loss, focus on what you require in order to take the first
step in the right direction. In taking that first step, you may find the
courage and confidence to take the next one.

Recognize your pain as significant but not insurmountable. When we
experience significant pain we may assume that it will never subside.
This assumption adds to the loneliness and helplessness that we already
feel and deepens our fear and anxiety. Although getting through loss is
difficult, most people find their way to that goal with time and effort.
Life going forward will probably remain difficult to some degree. Most

of us will never be completely free of the pain tied to our losses. We don't "get over" what we love and lose, at least not entirely. But we find ways to move through the most severe pain of loss so that it eventually subsides.

One of the more helpful things you can do is rely on others' encouragement. When you feel sad or despairing, you need encouragement that things will get better. One form of encouragement comes from your relationships with other people. You may surround yourself with persons who support you, and especially those who will tell you frequently that you will get through sadness and feel joy again. Consider spending time with those who make you think that better days lie ahead and look to those whom you can count on for encouragement.

At the same time, you will benefit as well from offering yourself support and encouragement. You may do this in many ways. One way is to say to yourself, perhaps out loud, several times a day, something like this: "The pain I feel right now will ease eventually. I can and will get through this. I know that things will improve." You may choose other words that feel more natural, or convincing, to you. Whatever the actual words, the idea is that some self-talk, even self-coaching, bears fruit.

Another twist on this approach involves choosing a few passages of Scripture that provide assurance and hope, and then reciting them multiple times during the day. You may also want to memorize and recite a quotation or two that provides encouragement to keep hoping. Find what works best and make use of it.

When we tell ourselves something over and over again, we tend to believe it. Our beliefs influence how we feel, think, and behave. If we tell ourselves that we will never be happy again, and will never experience any more joy and contentment, this is likely to prove true. But if we find ways to tell ourselves repeatedly that we will find happiness again, and that the future will be brighter, this will likely come to pass. Tell yourself that you will get through your loss. And ask someone who understands what you are going through to tell you this, too.

Remember that you are in the best position to discern how you feel, what you think, how you are behaving, and what you might need for your journey through loss. Nevertheless, there are some time-proven ways to facilitate this journey, and these are what I refer to as "good mourning." We will consider these in part 2, which focuses on the mourning process and its relationship to grief.

PART 2

So What?—Good Mourning

I will turn their mourning into joy, I will comfort them, and give them gladness for sorrow.

Jeremiah 31:13

Nothing can make up for the absence of someone whom we love, and it would be wrong to try to find a substitute; we must simply hold out and see it through. That sounds very hard at first, but at the same time it is a great consolation, for the gap, as long as it remains unfilled, preserves the bonds between us. It is nonsense to say that God fills the gap; he doesn't fill it, but on the contrary, he keeps it empty and so helps us to keep alive our former communion with each other, even at the cost of pain.

Dietrich Bonhoeffer, *Letters and Papers from Prison*

As we grieve, we appropriate new understandings of the world and ourselves within it. We also become different in the light of the loss as we assume a new orientation to the world.

Thomas Attig, *How We Grieve*

5

So What Does Mourning Require?

Getting through loss requires more than coping with grief. We also need to mourn what we have lost. Grief describes how we respond to loss, including how we feel, think, and behave. Mourning refers to the process whereby we loosen the emotional attachment (bond) to a loss, relocate the loss in our emotional life, and create emotional space for investing anew in relationships and other aspects of living. There is a lot of overlap between grief and mourning. The strategies for coping with loss during periods of grief apply to the mourning process as well. But good mourning requires an even more intentional and focused effort to cope with loss, and it calls upon us to do this in particular ways.

Unlike grieving, mourning does not happen on its own. It requires hard work and perseverance. It also requires time. Because mourning requires intentional focus and effort, most of us cannot begin to mourn immediately following a loss. We need time to come to terms with loss, express our pain, and get our bearings. Time also allows us to find a store of emotional, physical, and spiritual energy to draw upon as we mourn. This usually takes at least two or three months after a loss. So a good rule of thumb is that most people need a couple of months before they are ready to mourn in the ways I suggest here. Some will need to grieve even longer before mourning. Whatever its duration, a period of grief *prepares* us for mourning. This preparation involves coping with grief-related feelings, thoughts, and behaviors.

FIVE FEATURES OF GOOD MOURNING

It's rare for someone to identify a definitive point in time when she finished grieving and turned her attention exclusively to mourning. Typically, a bereaved person experiences a back-and-forth movement between grief and mourning for an extended period. So at any time following a loss you may find strategies for coping with loss (grieving) *and* strategies for mourning helpful.

Despite the overlap between grief and mourning, there are important differences between them. Making this distinction helps us in several ways. A focus on grief may help us understand what typically happens in loss and also what may help us to cope with our own losses. This is especially important for the first few days and weeks following the loss. A focus on mourning may help with this, too, but here we attend more explicitly to changing our relationship with what we lost. In mourning, we work to change this relationship in order to find more lasting relief and peace.

I suggest that there are five aspects of good mourning, or five things that help us mourn well: *receiving* our loss, *enduring* our loss, *adapting* to our loss, *relocating* our loss, and *sojourning* with our loss (when needed).[1] Let's examine how attending to each one promotes getting through loss in ways that foster comfort, health, wholeness, and peace.

Receiving Our Loss

Mourning well begins with "receiving" the loss that has occurred. Receiving involves two features: *acknowledgment* and *acceptance*. Both of these originate in the *grief* process, especially as we seek to cope with loss. As we grieve and cope, we attend to our feelings, thoughts, and behaviors in the wake of loss. This is when we need to begin to acknowledge the reality of the loss, for ourselves and others. We may move back and forth between acknowledging the loss and denying it. This is common for the first several days and, sometimes, longer. A back-and-forth movement serves a protective function. It allows us to receive the loss on our own terms, as we feel ready to take it on. But eventually, if we are to mourn, we need to acknowledge what we have lost.

In mourning we need to continue to acknowledge our loss, just as we did in grief. But we need to do something more. We need to *accept* the effects of loss, including its irreversible nature. A loved one has died, and we will not be reunited with her in the time we have remaining to us on this earth. A job has been lost and will not be ours again. A diagnosis has been made, and barring a miracle or misdiagnosis, we will not be free from disease. A marriage has ended, and we will not reconcile with our spouse. A dream has been quashed, never to be realized. Whatever the loss, we "receive" it by making a conscious, deliberate effort to recognize its reality (acknowledgment) and concede the lasting void that comes with it (acceptance). This acceptance includes awareness that life will not be the same as it was before the loss. Acceptance may begin as we grieve, but in mourning it intensifies and widens in scope.

Another way of thinking about receiving a loss is in terms of "owning" it. Owning a loss differs from being afflicted with loss or suffering loss. Affliction and suffering involve a degree of passivity and submissiveness. Here, loss and its effects lord over us, robbing us of joy and peace. While it is certainly true that loss can feel overpowering, to "receive" a loss involves a deliberate, active response to its power. To receive a loss means to take possession of it, as opposed to allowing it to possess us. When receiving a loss we resolve to confront its devastation and resist its crippling power. This is hard work.

In the next chapter, I suggest various strategies for mourning. Some of these will center on helping you receive your loss. You may discover additional strategies, and some of these may prove more helpful than the ones mentioned. Still, the basic idea here is to develop strategies that will help you. Either way, what is most important here is finding a way to confront your loss directly, so as not to avoid its reality or effects. These effects will not diminish because you dodge them.

Enduring the Loss

If we are able to acknowledge the reality of our loss and accept its effects, we are ready to "endure" the loss. There's no exact way to gauge this, but it helps to pay attention to a couple of things. First, are you able to verbalize, to yourself and to another person, that your loss has occurred? Can you say, "My friend has died" or "I have been fired from my job" or "My wife has left me" or "My dream of conceiving a child is over"? Second, in saying these things are you able to recognize the pain that your loss is causing you? Can you identify the hurt that your loss has brought? If you can answer yes to these questions, then you are likely to be ready to "endure" your loss.

Endurance means having the resolve to bear the brunt of the pain that the loss inflicts, and to do so for a substantial period of time. The amount of time will vary from person to person. For some, it will be a few days or weeks. For others, it will be a few months or longer. Whatever time it takes, your focus here needs to be on embracing the loss, indulging it even, and allowing its enormity to wash over you so that you truly feel its effects.

This may sound like an odd suggestion. Most of us naturally shun the pain of loss and seek to rid ourselves of it as soon as possible. We usually want nothing more than to put the loss behind us by letting go of the pain immediately. Couple these inclinations with the fact that most segments of society, including some of the people around us, encourage us to "move on." They want us to get through grief quickly, for their sake if not for ours. A minister I know recently told me about one of his parishioners' experiences after his wife died. The couple had been attached to a close-knit faith community. A year after his wife's death, this man was still weeping on a regular basis. Two elders in the community told him that he should no longer be crying over his wife's death, and left the man feeling guilty for doing so. Soon thereafter, the man withdrew from the community altogether.

This kind of "encouragement" to "move on" often stems from feeling uncomfortable with loss, and especially losses due to death. This discomfort contributes to related feelings of awkwardness. People who want to comfort someone who is grieving often don't know what to say. So they say something that, in effect, aims to get rid of their own discomfort. They say "It's time to get over it; time to 'move on.'" At the same time, one who grieves may not know what to say to those who attempt to offer comfort. The result may be that both grievers and comforters dismiss each other's feelings, change the subject, or offer some type of shallow platitude that neither person truly believes but that serves to fill the awkward silence nonetheless.

Here are some examples of such platitudes: "Don't worry, you'll be feeling better in no time. That's the way Harold would want it." "At least he went quickly and didn't suffer." "God must have needed her in heaven more than we needed her here." "Let's get your mind off this sad experience." "Think of all the fun you'll have being single again." "You've been sad long enough. It's time to put this behind you." People may have said similar things to you.

Although they maybe meant well, responses like these tend to hurt us more than they help. We hear in these responses that our grief is unwarranted, unacceptable, or unbecoming.[2] As a result, we begin feeling an obligation to "move on" or "to look on the bright side of things" as quickly as we can. This obligation can lead to cutting ourselves off from our grief-related feelings. We also may ignore how our grief impacts how we think and behave. Why? Because we think that we have to "move on."

How might you respond to well-intentioned, but unhelpful, things that people say after your loss? Here are some possibilities:

- "I hope that I will feel better eventually, but right now I feel _____ [you supply the feeling], and it's important for me to know this."
- "I am grateful that he did not suffer, but his 'going quickly' has left me feeling _____ [you supply the feeling], and I need to recognize this."
- "I don't find comfort in thinking that God would take my loved one to satisfy God's need in heaven" [if this is how you feel]. Or, "I'll have to talk to God about that. Right now, I can't help feeling that God has lots of helpers, and I need my one dearest friend so very much."
- "I can imagine that it will be helpful to get my mind off of things at some point. Right now, I think that my mind needs to be focused on this devastating [or whatever description you would offer] experience and the pain it has brought."
- "Maybe I will have fun someday as a result of being single again, but right now I feel _____ [you supply the feeling]."

If you don't feel comfortable saying this to the other person, say it to yourself.

The point to stress is that mourning requires that you defy assumptions and inclinations—others' and your own—that prevent you from feeling what you feel, thinking what you think, and acting as you need to act in the wake of a loss. You will need to push back against these assumptions and inclinations with gracious resolve. In order to get through loss, you will need to embrace its significance and pain to the fullest extent possible. "Moving on" is certainly the goal. But this requires the work of mourning, and mourning demands that you allow for your own experience. We need to allow ourselves truly to feel what we have lost and welcome our feelings (thoughts and behaviors too) long enough to confront the loss's power and effects. Only as we confront our experience and embrace it will it eventually run its course in ways conducive to mourning well.

To illustrate the value of allowing feelings to run their course, let's compare the pain of loss to the effects of a viral infection. When we have a viral infection, there is usually little that we can do to cure it other than simply letting it work itself through our system. Drinking plenty of fluids helps this process. So do rest and other kinds of care. Sometimes we will also use analgesics to control fever, aches, and pains. But doctors say that too much aspirin or Tylenol, while keeping the fever down, may actually prolong the viral illness. Why? Because a fever is the body's natural response to a viral infection. Running a fever has the effect of killing the virus. So while we may want to temper some of the fever's effects with analgesics, we need to allow the fever to run its course for health to improve.

Like a virus that needs to run its course, the feelings that we experience following a loss need to run their course. They need to be recognized, dealt with, and simply affirmed for what they are. We need to create a space for them and allow them to live in us on their terms. We certainly may care for ourselves and receive the care of others while we do this. We can make use of these "analgesics" to control the aches and pains that come our way. But we have to resolve to let our feelings "burn" for a while too. As with a fever when we're ill with a virus, diminishing the burn of these feelings by ignoring them will not make them go away. In fact, feelings associated with loss remain present even when we are unaware of them. When we don't allow them to run their course, they can intensify, stay with us longer, and become destructive.

Adapting to Loss

The loss of someone or something we love almost always forces significant changes in our lives. On a practical level, we are forced to alter our roles in the wake of loss. For example, we may have to assume the role of breadwinner, bill payer, financial planner, single parent, laundress, cook, gardener, or family chauffeur. On a deeper level, we no longer have the ability to talk face-to-face with a loved one who has died about our joys, problems, or dreams. Nor can we share routines of daily living, like meals, going to church, taking an evening walk, or shopping. Nor can we count on them to contribute what they once did to our happiness, sense of value, meaning, security, or self-understanding. Certainly, those we lose may still have some effect on our lives. People we love "live on" in us and among us in significant ways and contribute to our lives accordingly. But their presence in our lives will be different, and we now need to adapt to life without them.

Those who spend a lot of time caring for a chronically or terminally ill person often have difficulty adapting to the loss of that person. A caregiver's routine becomes tied to the daily needs and tasks of care. In many cases, so, too, does the caregiver's identity and self-understanding. Many people say things like: "I don't know what I will do with myself now that she's gone." "He doesn't need me to care for him anymore. So what's my purpose?" "It's so strange to have all of this free time now."

Other kinds of losses bring about different needs for adapting. The loss of a job requires adapting to unemployment, a lack of income, and the absence of former friends and colleagues. Perhaps losing a job also prompts the need to adapt to a new job or career that brings with it new people, routines, practices, and goals. The loss of a marriage to divorce usually requires adaptation with respect to matters of intimacy, economics, parenting, personal routines, and future plans. The same can be said about serious romantic relationships that end. Whatever our loss, we usually have to make substantial changes in several aspects of our lives. Life as we knew it changes forever.

We sometimes forget that losses also affect our identity and self-understanding. Our understanding of who we are and who we want to be forms in relationship to significant others in our lives. Parents, siblings, extended family members, close friends, colleagues, and other close associates contribute to our self-understanding simply because of their presence in our lives. They communicate their own self-understanding, values, goals, interests, and ways of living to us. These inevitably shape us and our lives. We shape others' lives, too, by communicating our self-understanding, values, goals, interests, and ways of living to them. You are who you are by virtue of loving, being loved by, and living in the presence of others and who they are. Because your self-understanding is tied so closely to your relationships, the loss of someone significant usually means losing a part of yourself as well. You hear people indicate this when they say things like "When he died [or left], part of me died too." Not only the loss of a person, but the loss of anything that brings you joy, safety, security, value, meaning, or self-understanding requires making substantial changes—adaptations—in your life.

Many of us will need to adapt to loss as it relates to our spiritual or religious lives. Loss can affect our sense of the cosmos, God, and the nature of God's relationship to us. Loss can raise questions about God's role in our lives and the created order. In most cases, loss prompts us to assess our spiritual lives, including our religious commitments and practices. We may think about the role that these have had in our life and may continue to have as we go forward. When I served as a pastor, I had numerous conversations with people that centered on more overt spiritual or religious concerns raised by an experience of loss.

I offer suggestions for adapting to loss in the next chapter. Here, I want to stress a few of the things that you can focus on as you begin to adapt. Remember that taking small steps is best. The journey through mourning requires taking steps to get through loss, but we cannot take every step at once. Sometimes those who mourn try to make too many changes too quickly in their lives. While they have good intentions in doing so, they often wind up frustrated if not overwhelmed. They sometimes make changes that they later regret.

Such changes may include getting rid of a deceased loved one's belongings right away or moving to another home. Other examples are getting romantically involved soon after the loss of a spouse or partner, or making an abrupt career change after losing a job. At some point, these kinds of changes may prove helpful, even necessary. But it is almost always best to spread changes over the course of several months or longer. Too much change too soon can complicate mourning.

You'll want to keep in mind that although loss may be devastating and present all kinds of difficulty, sometimes losses bring unforeseen opportunities and gains. Assuming new roles can feel empowering. New roles can enhance self-understanding, build confidence, and foster self-esteem. Each of these facilitates good mourning. Similarly, adapting to loss may present new insights related to God, your faith or spirituality, and how to foster deeper commitments to each.

At the same time, you need not feel pressure to "square" your loss with your spiritual or religious understandings or commitments. Perhaps this will occur eventually. Most people find that it does. Nevertheless, to force your experience into a "tidy" theological or spiritual perspective prematurely does more harm than good. God will journey with you through the mourning process at *your* pace. Accept this gracious gift and rely upon it.

Relocating the Loss

After receiving and enduring a loss for some time, we are ready to begin "relocating" it. Relocating a loss requires three things. First, we loosen bonds to what we have lost. Second, we withdraw some of the emotional energy tied to it. Third, we move what we have lost to a different emotional place. This process takes time and effort. You do not need to rush it.

As we begin to relocate a loss we usually experience two significant changes. First, we begin feeling more at peace with what we have lost. Why? Because we are gaining some emotional distance from it. We are freeing ourselves from some of the toll that loss takes. Second, we find energy for investing in new or renewed aspects of life, relationships, interests, and other passions. Loosening the bonds to what we have loved and lost and moving the loss to another emotional place often restores energy that we need in order to move through the pain of loss *and* experience life anew.

Loosening bonds does not mean severing them. Nor does moving what we have lost to a different emotional place mean that we no longer value it or want a relationship with it. We continue to love what we have lost. What happens in mourning is *not* that we cease to love, but that we find an appropriate place in our emotional lives for what we have loved and lost. When needed, we may go to this appropriate place to access the memories and emotions surrounding our loss. We may visit what we have lost—sojourning with it—after we have relocated it. But in moving a loss to another place, we create emotional space for nurturing other relationships and objects of affection. We may go to the special place of mourning when we want or have the need to. But we don't have to live in that place all the time. We can continue to love what we have lost without its remaining front and center in our lives. Sigmund Freud said it well: "We find a place for what we lose." Finding a place for what we have lost helps us mourn well.

Sojourning with the Loss (When You Need To)

I have already touched on the final feature of good mourning, namely, "sojourning" with a loss when we have the need. "Sojourning" means visiting or spending time somewhere. Often, sojourning involves resting and renwal. For these reasons, "sojourning" with what we have lost can help us mourn well. In mourning, our sojourn usually involves invoking memories of a life once shared with what we have lost. We may invoke these memories in different ways. When our loss is due to the death of a loved one, one way is to spend time in a place that was meaningful to our loved one. Tim recently lost his brother, Joe, who died suddenly. Tim "visits" Joe by going camping with friends every year, and also by attending professional football games of Joe's favorite team. Tim and Joe enjoyed sharing these activities for many years. Engaging in them now serves to tie the two together. Tim feels connected to Joe through memories of special times they shared. Tim visits Joe in other ways as well. But camping and attending football games provide Tim comfort and connection to what he has lost.

Sometimes we may prefer to sojourn with a loss by spending time alone. A leisurely walk, sitting in a quiet place, or going for a long drive may provide for such sojourning. Or we may sojourn when visiting a grave site or looking at pictures or other tokens of a life shared. Various faith rituals like prayer, Scripture reading, worship, and Communion also allow for sojourning with our loss.

Sometimes our sojourns involve efforts to help others. A primary example of this is a loss that sparks new interests and commitments to particular causes. We may become involved in movements or advocacy work relating to an illness or other circumstances linked to our loss. Advocacy also may tie to passions that a loved one had. Sometimes, for example, mourners get involved with Mothers Against Drunk Driving, the American Cancer Society, Alzheimer's support groups, suicide prevention and aftercare organizations, law enforcement benevolence work, organizations focused on reducing violence, job training and retraining agencies, single parenting networks, infertility care groups, and agencies that support adoption. This kind of involvement keeps the memory of what has been lost alive, whether a person, relationship, career, or dream. It's possible that overinvolvement in these sorts of organizations and activities may distract us from the pain of loss or the work of mourning.

But this involvement may also assign some sort of meaning to loss that comes with serving others and contributing to the common good. You will probably discover other ways to sojourn with your loss. These will become uniquely your own. They will reflect what you find most comforting, meaningful, and helpful for keeping your relationship with what you have lost alive. Sometimes the ways we visit our losses change over time. This is OK too. In fact, it may prove most helpful to sojourn in several ways and to mix them up from time to time. Think about what approaches could be most helpful, and sojourn consistently.

In the next chapter, I suggest several strategies that promote these five features of mourning. Before you continue reading, you may want to pause and think more about what could promote your own mourning as described here. Ask yourself what could help you receive, endure, adapt to, relocate, and sojourn with your loss.

6

So What Promotes Good Mourning?

When sustaining a difficult loss, we want to know how to manage our pain and feel better. This desire most likely led you to read this book. When we mourn we ask questions like: "What can I do to get through this loss?" "Is there any way to ease my pain?" "What am I to do now that I feel like my life is over?" These questions and others like them point to the difficulties posed by loss. Perhaps no life experience causes more pain. These questions also indicate that we usually feel that we need to *do* something to get through the pain of loss.

The five features of good mourning identify what we may do: we feel better as we receive, endure, adapt to, relocate, and sojourn with what we have lost.[1] But here are some additional things that we may do to mourn well. These strategies promote the five features of mourning, and help us manage our pain, get through our loss, and feel better.

STRATEGIES FOR MOURNING WELL

Remember that these strategies overlap with the strategies for coping mentioned previously (chapter 4). We probably never identify a definitive moment when we move from grieving to mourning. These two experiences remain fluid and overlap. We move back and forth between them as we seek to get through our losses. *Both* sets of strategies—those for coping with loss during grief and those for mourning—provide the assistance we need. Nevertheless, the following strategies are especially helpful for good mourning.

Tell yourself repeatedly that your loss has occurred (acknowledgment) and also that you need to go forward living with the void it has left (acceptance). Many people find it helpful to repeat certain phrases as a way to promote this self-talk. For example, you might say: "My mother has died. I need to live without her." "My marriage has ended. I am now single." "My spouse has an addiction. Our lives are different now." "We are infertile. Our plans to conceive a child have changed." "I've lost my job. I'm now unemployed." "My relationship has ended. I have to begin anew." You will think of other phrases to repeat in light of your loss, and your need to acknowledge and accept it.

Note here the importance of the language used. Many of us avoid speaking candidly about loss. In terms that Martin Luther used, we often steer clear of words that "call a thing what it is." We evade terms like "death" and "died." We opt instead for expressions like "passed away," "passed on," or "entered into glory." In the same way, we might say "laid off" or "resigned" to describe getting fired from a job. We might say that we are "splitting up" or "separating" from our spouse, even when we know that a divorce is imminent. Likewise, we sometimes soft-peddle an addiction, referring to it as "drinking too much" or "overindulging in alcohol." While different cultures and groups approach these matters in varying ways, most experts recognize the value of appealing to more direct, even blunt, language, particularly when working to receive and endure a loss.

Dare to use words like "dead," "fired," "divorce," and "addicted" when speaking of your loss. Using these words fosters acknowledgment, reception, and endurance of a loss because you have named its unvarnished presence in your life. Think of how you may name your loss with candor.

Make use of rituals that encourage confronting your loss. I have already noted the value of funerals. One way to deal with the effects of funerals that take place too soon is to draw on other rituals that provide similar benefits. There is merit in having a service of remembrance between six months and one year after a funeral. Such a service presents opportunities for mourning that were not experienced at the funeral. Visiting a grave site or place where ashes were deposited also proves helpful for some people. These visits serve to reinforce the fact of loss and its effects. In a similar way, looking at photographs or other meaningful mementos from a life once shared can simultaneously provide comfort and confirmation of loss.

Keeping meaningful family rituals alive, like holiday activities or birthday practices, may also prove helpful. Some families provide a place setting and keep an empty chair at the dinner table as a memorial for a loved one. Sometimes, surviving family members continue taking vacations and visiting places that they visited when their loved one was alive. Another common practice involves marking the anniversary of the death, or the deceased person's birthday, with a special ceremony or activity.

Mourning requires that we remind ourselves of what we have lost. Although painful and at times seemingly "unnatural," facing loss is better than ducking its effects. Confronting loss face-to-face, on a regular basis, is necessary. All of the ritual practices that I have mentioned can help with this.

Seek support from your minister, faith community, and others who care for you. I have already noted the value of talking about your loss with your minister, spiritual director, or others in your faith community. Find ways to do this regularly for several months after your loss. Most faith communities and ministers offer adequate support and care at the time a loss occurs. In the case of a loved one's death, most ministers and faith communities shower those who grieve with attention and encouragement, offering assistance with meals, errands, and other types of needs. This care and attention usually lasts for a few days to a week following the loss.

Ministers and faith communities usually intend to provide adequate longer-term care and support, but typically their efforts fall short. They are well-intentioned and caring people. They don't purposefully neglect the needs of the bereaved. But like most of us, caregivers get busy with their own lives. They are also called upon to respond to other concerns and more immediate needs for care and support. Sometimes they simply assume that the acute period of pain has passed after a few weeks' time.

The majority of people say that they benefit from support that comes several weeks after their loss. This is when they look to their faith community for help and need their minister's presence most. It takes a few weeks to begin "waking up" from the shock of loss. With this awakening comes more profound pain. Welcome your minister or other caregivers from your faith community whenever they extend offers to visit you. Even when this feels difficult, and it sometimes does, their support usually helps. But also consider requesting regular visits from them, especially for the first six months to one year following your loss.

Dare to be alone. Mourning also requires that we spend some time alone. For some of us, this comes naturally. Solitude is a significant part of our lives, whether during times of joy or of sorrow. We need time alone in order to think, feel, and recharge. For others of us, being alone comes less naturally; it may be something we shun. If so, we may find it particularly difficult to be alone as we mourn.

But spending some time alone can foster good mourning. Having time by yourself, away from the people and demands of daily life, can provide the focus and energy you need to mourn. Whether you seek to receive, endure, adapt to, relocate, or sojourn with a loss, finding a measure of solitude may provide the energy and focus you need.

Sometimes, people who offer us care assume that we should *not* be alone. Well-meaning friends and family members may seek to keep us "occupied" or "busy" in the hope that this will spare us some of the pain of loss. But too many distractions from our pain, and also from discerning what we need to move forward, will almost always prolong pain and intensify it.

Prepare yourself for the need to spend time alone as you mourn, and share this need with others who may not understand. You will probably benefit from finding a place of quiet and going there regularly as you mourn. You may spend five minutes at a time there, or you may even stay five hours at a time, depending on what works best for you. As the psalmist recalled, "They were glad because they had quiet, and he brought them to their desired haven" (Ps. 107:30).

Continue to identify your feelings, thoughts, and behaviors, but now assign them a value. One way to focus attention on how you feel, think, or behave is to identify your feelings, thoughts, and behaviors as specifically as possible and then assign them a value. While you may benefit from doing this fairly soon after your loss occurs, as you begin to grieve, this strategy may be especially helpful for mourning. Why? Because in mourning you need to pay closer attention to how your feelings, thoughts, and behaviors change over the course of time. You also need to understand how different people and places that you come in contact with affect how you feel, think, and behave. This attention and understanding help you identify what you are doing, or not doing, to promote good mourning.

Assigning a "value" to your feelings, thoughts, and behaviors is one way to pay closer attention to them and understand them better. "Value" here does not mean "good" or "bad," "noble" or "ignoble." Rather, value has to do with things like "intensity," "frequency," and "duration." Using a 1 to 5 scale, with 1 signifying "little intensity" and 5 signifying "great intensity," you can try to gauge the degree to which you feel what you feel. You could do the same with the categories of "frequency" and "duration." Some examples of feelings that you may identify as you mourn include sadness, anger, anxiety, and confusion. You may identify other feelings, too, but let's focus on these. Consider each of these feelings, one at a time. As you do so, assign a value to them.

Let's first consider the intensity of your feelings. Maybe it would play out like this: sadness = 5; anger = 2; anxiety = 1; and confusion = 3. If so, you might decide to "track" your feelings over the course of a couple of days, maybe longer, to see if and how they change in intensity. Keep two goals in mind. The first is to gain more of a sense of what you are experiencing—in this case, what you feel. You could practice a similar strategy of assigning value to how you think and behave too. In those cases, you might focus more on "frequency" or "duration." Or you may opt for another focus. The point is that honing your understanding of how you feel, think, and behave, and finding ways to track these responses over time, helps with the five features of mourning.

A second goal is to gauge how particular people, places, situations, and actions affect your feelings, thoughts, and behaviors—whether positively or negatively. Being in the presence of certain people can serve to intensify or lessen feelings of sadness, for example. Particular situations have a tendency to bring about confusion or frustration. Likewise, going to certain places can affect how anxious you feel.

Once you begin identifying and assigning "value" to your feelings, thoughts, and behaviors, you do well to share the findings with a confidant. This may be a minister or other spiritual friend. It could be a counselor or therapist. It could be someone else who provides comfort and support. Sharing your findings provides yet another opportunity for honing self-awareness as you mourn. Your confidant may also offer additional suggestions for how to get through your loss.

Identify changes you need to make to adapt to your loss, but prioritize them.
Mourning well requires adapting to your loss. Adapting involves making changes in your life. But it's usually best not to make too many changes too quickly. And various types of losses call for different changes. For example, adapting to the loss of a job requires life changes that differ from those needed for adapting to the loss of a family member or the dream of conceiving a child. Nevertheless, most significant losses require you to adapt in some fashion. Most losses prompt a need for some sort of change in your life.

You may feel tempted to identify all the changes you need to make to facilitate adapting to your loss. You may also be eager to implement these changes. Such desires are understandable and even welcome. We should never underestimate the positive role that our motivation to get through a loss can play in mourning well.

Changing too much too soon, however, almost always causes problems in mourning. You probably don't have enough energy to give to every change that you think you need to make. Even if you did have the energy, other factors (e.g., a lack of knowledge, understanding, or money) may prevent certain changes at the present time. To identify needed changes usually proves helpful, but prioritize these changes and implement them at a reasonable pace. Counselors often speak of "partializing" what needs attention. Partializing involves setting priorities for change and implementing changes accordingly.

Consider this brief example. Someone who loses a job probably needs to change several things about his current situation in order to adapt to the loss. Let's assume he needs to obtain some additional job training to stay in the same field. Let's assume, too, that if he were to change careers, he would need even more education or training. Let's also assume he needs to find a source of income, update his résumé, obtain help with restructuring debt, and buy new clothes to wear on job interviews. We might assume, too, that his family would benefit from his wife's securing employment outside the home, and from the couple beginning supportive counseling. The counseling would aim to help with the stress surrounding the job loss and its strain on the marriage.

All of these needs are significant. But think about what it would take to address all of them at the same time. This would be next to impossible, and the attempt would be grueling. Only the person experiencing the job loss (along with his family) would know what needs priority and how to proceed. But he should prioritize the needed changes and make them one or two at a time.

Cultivate a "place" for what you have lost. This strategy helps especially with "relocating" your loss and "sojourning" with it when needed. Remember that you relocate losses *not* to "let them go," but rather to create a new kind of relationship with them. At the same time, relocating losses allows room in your emotional life for forming and nurturing *new* relationships and passions. In finding a special "place" of mourning, you may travel there in your memories and imagination when needed. As you do so, you begin relating differently to what you have lost. It remains a part of you. But it does not stay in the forefront of your mind all the time. Nor does it dominate your emotional, relational, or spiritual life. As a result, you begin experiencing life anew. You free yourself for living and loving because you have reduced the burdens of loss.

We cultivate this mourning space in an almost unlimited number of ways. Someone I know, Lupe, spends ten or fifteen minutes each morning reminiscing about the life she once shared with her now-deceased husband. As she reflects in this place of mourning, she experiences sorrow and joy, tears and laughter, appreciation and regret. Different mornings bring different experiences. She finds this routine helpful, however, for several reasons. It gives her regular time with what she has lost. As each day begins, she travels to the "sacred" place in her memories to "meet" her husband. This helps her maintain her sense of connection to him. Her connection provides comfort and meaning. It also helps her find distance from the burdens that mourning otherwise places on her. She describes her experience in this way: "Waking up each day to spend time with Rafael brings me comfort and peace, even when I'm also sad. I have to do this if I'm to go on."

Lupe still has difficult days. Finding a special place of mourning does not provide a cure-all from pain. But having transferred Rafael's presence in her life largely to this "place" allows her to spend time there (sojourn)—*with* him—on her own terms, *when she wants or needs to do so.* Having a special place of mourning frees her from some of the pain that she experienced before finding this place and, presumably, from the pain that she would experience now if she did not have it.

James spends many weekends fishing at a nearby lake. He has experienced numerous losses in his life and says that he finds "solace," "connection," and "God" when he is on the water. When he feels particularly "down," "sad," or "angry," he tries to go fishing, and this usually helps him feel better.

Latisha lost her adolescent daughter to suicide. She absorbs herself in advocacy for suicide prevention and follow-up care. She says that she "finds peace" in this and keeps her daughter "close."

Michelle's young son died from leukemia. She now donates blood and platelets regularly, and she works diligently to support cancer research. She has become a champion of efforts to raise money and public awareness concerning cancer. Michelle recognizes that these efforts link her to her beloved son, even in his death. She also realizes that these efforts allow her to invest her feelings, thoughts, and behaviors in "resolving" her loss. She says, "I feel like I'm doing something important in this work, which keeps Billy close to me. It also helps me feel like his death had meaning for others." Michelle further notes that helping others affected by cancer brings its own kind of solace. In her mind, her work takes her to a different place—a different state of emotional, relational, and spiritual well-being. All of this, she indicates, helps her mourn well.

You will probably discover your own ways of cultivating a place for what you have lost. Rehearsing several of the other strategies for grieving and mourning may help you with this goal. Paying particular attention to physical settings that have been meaningful to you or to the one you have lost may help in cultivating your "place" of mourning. Some will want to spend time by water or in the mountains. Others will seek a church sanctuary, long walks in the woods, or a place to listen to music. Some may want to make quilts, paint, or garden. For some, spending time on the golf course has proved helpful. Any of these activities can help cultivate a special emotional, physical, and even spiritual space for mourning.

You also may benefit from the sorts of rituals already mentioned, like looking at pictures, watching videos that contain images of the person or thing you have lost, and also praying or meditating. You may find it helpful to record various aspects of your experience of loss, whether in poetry, journals, or some other medium. Other artistic outlets, such as drawing, painting, sculpture, pottery, and playing a musical instrument, can also help with creating the space needed to relocate a loss.

No one but you can say for sure what "place" you should choose or how specifically you should go about choosing it. The important thing is to identify ways to keep the memories of what you have lost "alive" and a *part* of you, while not allowing the loss to consume *all* of you. You want to find places—whether physical, emotional, spiritual, or some combination of these—that seem to welcome you as you mourn. There, you may feel, think, and act as you wish. Visit these places when life beckons you there. But it's important not to stay there all the time. The goal is to invest in life anew. Although in almost every case "you'll know it when you find it," it's important to work on finding your place.

Consider the benefits of new opportunities, interests, roles, relationships, and goals that present themselves. Sometimes loss brings about opportunities for making positive changes. In recognizing this potential, I'm not minimizing the pain of loss, nor do I suggest that loss is "good" or "positive" in itself. It may eventually become possible, however, to distinguish between the awfulness of loss and the opportunity for good in your life that may come about as a result. This is what the apostle Paul had in mind when he wrote, "We know that all things work together for good for those who love God, who are called according to his purpose" (Rom. 8:28). Paul does not suggest here that all things are "good," but that good can and does come out of terrible things.

It can prove helpful in mourning to focus attention on new opportunities and other benefits that come your way following loss. If your loss relates to retiring from public work, you may think about how the extra time you now have could be spent on travel, hobbies, serving the poor, mentoring younger persons, or other interests. When Jack retired from his job at age seventy, he and Grace spent three months a year traveling to places that they had always wanted to visit. Most were relatively close to home, but once a year they took a trip to what they called "a faraway place," sometimes even going abroad.

If your loss is the death of your spouse, you may consider what interests you may now explore that you could not pursue when your spouse was alive. Maybe you want to further your education. Perhaps you want to get more involved in your faith community or a local charity. Possibly you can now take over responsibility for finances, cooking, or other household duties that you enjoy and find meaningful. A few months after Marshall's death, Ruby got more involved with a local food bank. She worked there several hours each week and also volunteered at two homeless shelters that the food bank served. "I'd always wanted to do this," she said, "and Marshall wanted me to, but I just never found the time before he died. This work has been a blessing for me, and I know that Marshall would be happy to see me doing it, too."

It could be that you are mourning a loss of mobility due to deteriorating health. Although this certainly presents challenges and burdens, perhaps it also affords an opportunity to focus energy on reading, writing, playing with grandchildren, talking on the telephone, using the computer to pursue interests, or other things that you can do at home. Many people have found creative ways to reach out to others and support them after becoming less mobile and more homebound. Examples of this include sending greeting cards that mark various life events and occasions, whether joyful or painful; engaging regularly in prayer for and with others, whether in person, on the phone, or even by e-mail; sewing baby quilts; helping to prepare tax returns; writing letters to missionaries around the world; raising money for charities over the phone; and assisting children with homework after school. Though the increasing lack of mobility is unwelcome, you may discover that it brings some benefits and new opportunities. Assuming new roles and responsibilities can prove empowering and gratifying. Both usually contribute to good mourning.

Remind yourself that you will mourn in ways distinctly your own. You receive a great gift in mourning when you remember that no two persons mourn in exactly the same way. We all experience loss in distinct ways, even when we share certain aspects of loss. If you begin thinking that you have to mourn in a certain way, even in the ways set forth in this book, you set yourself up for more pain and complications. The same is true if you assume that you need to mourn within certain time constraints, or that you only mourn well by imitating the experiences of other bereaved persons.

Two years after her husband died, and after she remarried, Gracie would awaken every morning, sit on the edge of the bed, and cry for half an hour. Then she would get up, get dressed, and go to work. Her "morning cry" was part of a journey through mourning that worked for her. She felt better after crying, and was able to function well the remainder of the day. Mourning happens differently for different people.

So the mourning strategies that I have proposed serve only as a general map for navigating your own journey through loss. No one travels the same road through loss as another. Nor do we travel at the same pace. But if you attend to your grief-related feelings, thoughts, and behaviors, and to the five features of mourning that I have presented, you will find your own road and an appropriate pace to travel it.

Seek to deepen your faith in God and God's provision. This strategy is the subject of the next two chapters, where I suggest the role that faith can play in mourning and how various faith practices may help you mourn.

7

So What Role Can Faith Play?

In this chapter we pay closer attention to the relationship between loss and our spiritual lives. I suggest how Christian faith offers a basis for good mourning, and how certain faith practices foster mourning with hope and spiritual vitality.

When referring to "Christian faith," this is what I have in mind: *The story of God's transforming and redemptive work in human lives and all of creation through the life, death, and resurrection of Jesus and the ongoing work of the Holy Spirit.*[1] For more than two thousand years, Christians have encountered this story in the Bible and the church. Christians have also lived this story. In doing so, this gospel story has provided a guiding perspective on life, death, and hope for the future. We who seek to follow Jesus claim the Christian faith as our own. We seek to live our lives *within* this story. As a result, we allow this story to form us, transform us, and guide us in all facets of living. When we suffer loss, we do well to reflect on our experience in light of this story and the support and hope that it offers.

GOD, FAITH, AND LOSS

The Christian faith suggests a powerful link between our own suffering and God's suffering. We see this link especially in Jesus' suffering on our behalf. Numerous Christian writers throughout history have noted the importance of our identifying with Jesus, and his identifying with us, in suffering. Beginning with Paul and the New Testament writings, many people have pondered this idea of God suffering *with* human beings in the person of Jesus, and have underscored its significance for a faithful life. While suffering in a German prison during Nazi rule, theologian Dietrich Bonhoeffer described God's presence in human suffering. He writes: "God let himself be pushed out of the world on to the cross. He is weak and powerless in the world, and that is precisely the way, the only way, in which he is with us and helps us. Matt. 8:17 makes it quite clear that Christ helps us, not by virtue of his omnipotence, but by virtue of his weakness and suffering."[2] The passage from Matthew's Gospel that Bonhoeffer cites recalls Jesus' many acts of healing, when people brought infirm people to him and he "cured all who were sick" (v. 16). The Gospel writer notes that "this was to fulfill what had been spoken through the prophet Isaiah, 'He took our infirmities and bore our diseases'" (v. 17).

Bonhoeffer and the Gospel writer recognize God's promise to abide with us. In numerous places in Scripture, we are told that God pledges to remain present with God's people. Recall just a few examples. As Isaac prepared to enter Egypt, the Lord cautioned him against this, saying, "Reside in this land as an alien, and I will be with you, and will bless you" (Gen. 26:3). As Moses was dying, God spoke to Joshua and offered assurance of God's provision: "Then the LORD commissioned Joshua son of Nun and said, 'Be strong and bold, for you shall bring the Israelites into the land that I promised them; I will be with you'" (Deut. 31:23). After "the LORD made her conceive, and she bore a son[,] . . . the women said to Naomi, 'Blessed be the LORD, who has not left you this day without next-of-kin; and may his name be renowned in Israel! He shall be to you a restorer of life and a nourisher of your old age; for your daughter-in-law who loves you, who is more to you than seven sons, has borne him'" (Ruth 4:13–15). Furthermore, the prophet Isaiah declared on God's behalf, "'You [Israel] are my servant, I have chosen you and not cast you off'; do not fear, for I am with you, do not be afraid, for I am your God; I will strengthen you, I will help you, I will uphold you with my victorious right hand" (Isa. 41:9–10). And of course, we need to recall Jesus' parting words to his disciples as recounted in Matthew's Gospel: "Remember, I am with you always, to the end of the age" (Matt. 28:20).

We take these assurances from God's promise: God suffers as Jesus suffers on our behalf, and God suffers with *us* when we suffer. Suffering with us, God does not abandon us to face suffering alone. God pledges over and over again: "I will be with you." As we endure the pain of loss, we can take heed of God's promise that provides hope. This hope stems from confidence that no less than God recognizes us in our suffering, and no less than God suffers along with us.

Identifying with the suffering of Jesus in particular may help us place more trust in God as we mourn. Like Jesus, we are recognized by God. As with Jesus, God has pledged to be with us at all times. Jesus' story thus becomes our story. As a result, our painful experiences have deeper significance than they otherwise would have. Jesus has walked where we now tread; just as God was there with him, so God is here with us. Sharing Jesus' story, we may mourn what we have lost with courage and hope. Why? Because as with Jesus, God promises that our suffering does not have the final say. Like Jesus, we may hope for a personal future when our pain is swallowed up and we shall mourn no more.

HOW FAITH PRACTICES MAY HELP YOU

How might we sharpen awareness of God's abiding presence in our lives, especially during times of loss? How can we cultivate trust in God and reliance upon God's promises, particularly as we mourn? Furthermore, what helps us rely on other people, especially those with whom we share faith, in getting through our loss? An answer to all three of these questions is this: We can participate in faith practices that Christianity offers.

Faith practices are specific *activities* bound to our faith that we may engage in routinely; activities like church membership, worship, Scripture reading, service to others, and prayer. There are other practices, of course, and you are encouraged to consider them and their meaningfulness to you and your particular tradition. But I will limit the focus here to the ones mentioned.

These activities—practices—provide at least three things that we need as we mourn. This first is a deeper connection to God and others, especially those in the faith community. Second, faith practices promote a regular encounter with the Christian story, including its promises. Third, as we engage them, faith practices draw us deeper into this story, its claims, and what it says about life, death, and hope for the future. Faith practices bind us to the Christian story. In doing so, faith practices call upon us to consider all of our experiences, including loss, in light of the Christian faith and the support and hope that it imparts.

FIVE FAITH PRACTICES THAT PROMOTE GOOD MOURNING

These five faith practices can help with mourning: church membership, worship, reading Scripture, serving others, and prayer. The practice of prayer will be considered separately in the next chapter. You will discover the best way to engage these practices, and others like them, as they become part of your life. Some of these may be part of your life already, or were part of it at some earlier time. These practices take different forms, and you may engage them in various ways. You will need to figure out what helps most with mourning. *Only you* can do this for yourself. But these practices provide a good place to begin.

Church Membership

It may not typically be thought of in this way, but membership in a faith community—a church—is a faith practice. Church membership asks certain things of us. Membership also holds us accountable, to some extent, for meeting its requirements. Church membership likewise calls upon us to be active in a shared life and mission. We expect all members to contribute to church life while also taking from it in appropriate ways. Our mutual accountability and contributions bind us in distinctive ways to God, the Christian faith, other persons, and the world. Most people say that active church membership makes a significant difference in their lives.

For many of us, belonging to a congregation affects various aspects of life. These include our relationships, values, goals, self-understanding, sense of meaning and purpose, plans for the future, hope, and trust. Being part of a faith community—bound to others in Christ—shapes how we feel, think, and act concerning all manner of things. If you don't belong to a congregation, perhaps you can at least imagine that this would have a positive effect on your life.

In times of loss, membership in the church can provide for several needs. Among the more immediate ones is the need for *connection*. Loss usually makes us feel somewhat isolated and *dis*connected. When suffering loss we can feel cut off from other people and, perhaps, from God. As a result, we may feel anxious, afraid, vulnerable, or confused. We also may feel hopeless, and wonder how we can ever feel whole and at peace again. Having a sense of connection to God and other people can keep feelings of isolation and related struggles at bay.

We also stand in need of comfort, encouragement, and companionship in times of loss. We need to feel that we *belong*—to others, but especially to God. A sense of belonging is perhaps the strongest kind of connection. This helps us meet our deepest needs. Furthermore, sensing that we belong, especially to God, helps hone our awareness of God's abiding presence. This awareness helps us cultivate trust in God. As we trust in God, we rely ever more on God's promises. We also tend to rely more on other people, our companions in faith, and this reliance adds to our sense of connection and belonging. At the same time, belonging to a congregation encourages us to engage in other faith practices. These draw us further into the Christian story and call upon us to take part in it.

Reliance on others in the faith community becomes especially valuable when we experience spiritual fatigue. On these occasions, we may rest in the comfort of others' prayers and faith practices. We can let go of worries or guilt that stem from not being able to pray, or get ourselves to worship, or trust in God's provision. We can let go of these because we have the community on which to rely. The community—the body of Christ—prays, worships, and even believes on our behalf when we cannot do these things ourselves. It is the role and duty of the faith community to embrace us in these ways when we struggle and cannot practice our faith as we otherwise would.

Joining a faith community may feel difficult to do. So, too, may increasing your present level of commitment where you already belong. These may fall a long way down on the list of what you feel like trying, given your pain and lack of energy. Still, it's usually worth doing your best to invest in church life. The sense of belonging that follows nourishes deep connections with God and others. Through these connections, God will be with you in a tangible way. Sensing God's presence amid your connections to others provides a basis for meeting many needs as you mourn.

Worship and Reading Scripture

Worship and reading Scripture may also help you with good mourning. Although distinct, these two practices have several things in common when it comes to their effects on those who engage in them. I ask that you consider these practices in light of their similar capacities to shape how you feel, think, and act in life, especially in times of mourning.

Acts of worship and reading Scripture enrich the way we live. Most people who practice them will note their effects. Those who practice them regularly will attest to their capacity to change lives. Let's consider three ways that these practices may affect mourning.

Worship and reading Scripture draw us more deeply into the Christian story. I have spoken of the Christian faith in terms of a story. It is the story of God's transforming and redemptive work in human lives and all of creation through the life, death, and resurrection of Jesus and the ongoing work of the Holy Spirit. This story conveys God's nature, and speaks of God's provision and desires for all people. This story also tells of how God, especially as known in the person of Jesus, comforts, heals, renews, and restores health, wholeness, relational well-being, and spiritual vitality. The Christian story is about God's love for all people, including you.

Living with this story shapes how we feel and think about life and death, and also our hopes for the future. This story also affects how we act. Why? Because through encountering this story, we encounter God. Bonhoeffer put it this way:

> It is not that God is the spectator and sharer of our present life, howsoever important that is; but rather that we are the reverent listeners and participants in God's action in the sacred story, the history of the Christ on earth. And only in so far as we are *there*, is God with us today also.[3]

When we embrace the Christian story, make it our own, and seek to live it, we encounter God. Encountering God, we feel, think, and act in light of what the gospel story declares *about* God, Jesus, ourselves, and our neighbors. We could go as far as to say that we live *within* the story. We become part of the story because it has become a deep part of us. It forms, transforms, and guides us. It leads to more intimacy with God. It draws us toward Jesus and the life he modeled. The story provides, too, for understanding ourselves and our needs, and it hones our sensitivity to the needs of others. This story of God's love invites our participation, for our own sake and the sake of the world.

We encounter and participate in the Christian story through worship and reading the Scriptures. Here we meet God. Here God meets us. In worship we listen to the Christian story told, over and over again, *through* the Scriptures. We also engage in various rituals like baptism, Communion, ordination, and the laying on of hands. Through these rituals, and in our prayers, singing, service, and the sharing of our lives with others, we not only encounter the Christian story, we participate in it.

For Christians, living within this story can become normative for life. This story affects our experiences, relationships, and actions. It is not that we live apart from the Christian story and then ask what that story might say to us about our lives. We have already been taken into the story through faith. We have already claimed the story and recognized its claims on us. As a result, we ask what difference this story makes on how we experience life and understand it. On occasions of loss, we are invited to perceive our experience and need in light of the Christian faith, its support, and its hope. To that end, worship and reading Scripture draw us into the Christian story, keep us there, and sustain us with its promises.

Worship and reading Scripture foster ongoing connections to God and other people in community. I have noted how loss can make you feel alone, abandoned, and cutoff from other people and God. Those who grieve or mourn may say things like: "I feel so lonely." "My friends and family seem so distant now." "Hard as I try, I just don't want to be with people." "I don't feel like God is with me anymore."

You may have said some of these things yourself. If so, know that you are not strange. This is not kooky behavior; it is rather typical. Furthermore, you may very well benefit from time alone, away from others, for a period. If you feel that this will do you some good, then allow it. Listen to yourself and discern what you need. But eventually you need to find ways to reconnect with others and renew your most significant relationships. You will benefit from the presence and support of loved ones as you mourn what you have lost.

Church membership itself provides for strong connections to God and other persons. But central to church membership are the practices of worshiping God and reading the Scriptures with companions in faith. We may engage in these faith practices alone. Many of us find it meaningful to read the Bible and spend time with God by ourselves, in a posture of worship. But we also need to do these things with others as part of a faith *community*.

Jesus' first followers engaged in these practices with one another regularly: "They devoted themselves to the apostles' teaching and fellowship, to the breaking of bread and the prayers" (Acts 2:42). Even more than two thousand years later, nothing substitutes for Christians' assembling together to engage in acts of worship. As we worship *together*, listen to the Scriptures being read *together*, pray *together*, and engage in other types of meaningful rituals *together*, we live the Christian story *together*. In living this story with one another, we find ourselves bound to God, each other, and the world in ways that only come with *sharing* a worshipful life.

You may be skeptical about these claims. When I served as pastor of a congregation, I heard people say with confidence on more occasions than I can recall that they were just fine with a "private spiritual life." I heard people say: "I can worship God at home, by myself. That's what I like." Or, "I worship God every Saturday morning on the golf course. I find peace there." Or, "I'm not for organized religion. I'm spiritual, but my relationship with God is a personal thing." Certainly many people believe this. Furthermore, faith communities don't always seem inviting. They are not as hospitable as they could be. A popular bumper sticker notes the church's imperfections with candor: "I love God. It's his fans that I can't stand."

But one's relationship with God cannot be entirely personal or private. Our relationship with God surely unfolds in solitude with God. Some of us may indeed experience this kind of solitude on the golf course, at home, or in nature. But our relationship with God also unfolds when it is lived out with others who seek to live the Christian story themselves. We live the faith most fully when we embrace its principles and practices with others who are seeking to do the same.

Here's an analogy that illustrates the difference between engaging in faith practices alone and with other persons. I love writing. I like the challenge, investment, discipline, and artistry involved with sitting down at my laptop computer consistently and trying to get my ideas on paper. This never happens with ease. Just the opposite; it is always difficult work. But writing holds a central place in my life, and I miss it when I'm away from it for long.

Anyone who writes will tell you that it is largely a solitary endeavor. You find a quiet place to sit with your ideas, nurture them while they mature, and then give birth to them in written form. Even if you write in a public place—like a coffee shop or park bench—you still do it more or less alone. It has to be this way.

Nevertheless, the best writing requires that we eventually invite others to join us. We produce the most meaningful and highest quality of work as we share it with others. I am thinking here not only of the final product, but also the process of writing. We benefit from the wisdom, insight, and company of trusted friends, colleagues, editors, and even critics. We may forgo inviting others into our process of writing; some people probably do. But if I did that, I am certain that my work would suffer. I learn a lot from what others say about my writing. Whether supportive or critical, this proves invaluable. Furthermore, I would miss out on the inspiration and joy that comes with sharing my work with others and hearing how it has affected them (or not). Other people see things differently than I do. They have alternative takes on matters, different assumptions and biases. Sometimes these alternative perspectives serve to alter my own, and sometimes not. Nevertheless, when I invite others to share their perspectives on what I have written, this sharing almost always leads to richer understandings of my own perspectives. This makes for better writing. Nothing substitutes for this kind of sharing in the practice of writing.

In a similar way, the practices of worship and reading Scripture—like all faith practices—happen best when they happen at least part of the time with other people. We can engage in them alone. We may find benefits in doing so. But they are usually most meaningful and enriching when we also engage in them with companions. These people not only share our interests and life, but they may have alternative perspectives that enrich our own. Few things that enhance life happen exclusively alone. Certainly this is the case for worship and reading Scripture. God's "fans" will prove maddening at times. But living your faith with others *will* enrich your life.

Worship and reading Scripture transport us to spiritual and emotional places where we may mourn. Let's return to the need to create and cultivate new "places" or "spaces" for mourning. We find comfort, rest, encouragement, and hope in these places. We also may find there a deeper connection with God, other people, and the Christian story.

Worship and reading Scripture nurture these very connections. Our connections ease our sense of vulnerability and anxiety. They also strengthen our sense of safety and security, which has been threatened by an experience of loss. Because of the connections these places foster, they become sacred. We learn to rely on the opportunities we have to enter them as we have need. We also trust that we will find in them sustenance for the journey through loss.

Three Steps for Making Worship and Scripture Reading a Central Part of Your Life

As is true with other faith practices, you will discover the best ways to make Scripture reading and worship central to your life. But consider the following three steps.

Step 1: Worship and read Scripture often. Think about worshiping at least once a week, and more if possible. Many faith communities offer midweek services consisting of prayer, healing rituals, Bible study, and other faith practices. These services often have an intimate feel. This intimacy in itself may offer you comfort and support.

Also, commit to reading Scripture *every day.* You may find it helpful to purchase a Bible that sets forth a pattern of daily reading that will allow you to read the entire Bible in one year. Or you may decide to follow a schedule of readings (called the lectionary), which many denominations publish (see page 102 for information). You also could choose particular biblical books to read, and reread, over time.

Whatever route you take, include readings from the Psalms in your daily practice. Psalms of lament may prove especially helpful. These include Psalms 3–7, 10–14, 16, 17, 22, 23, 25–28, 31, 35, 36, 38, 39, 51–59, 61–64, 69, 71, 73, 86, 88, 102, 109, and 130.[4] Read the entire collection of psalms often. But remember that the lament psalms especially tend to resonate with people who mourn. These psalms express the depths of human pain and include requests for God's intervention.

Bonhoeffer points out that the book of Psalms consists entirely of prayers. He called the Psalms the prayerbook of the Bible.[5] He points out that these were the Scriptures and prayers that Jesus knew and recited, and that as we pray these prayers ourselves, we join Jesus in prayer.

Consider taking part in regular worship and Scripture reading. Begin doing it now, and stay with it. This will enrich your faith. At the same time, you will discover help for good mourning.

Step 2: Consider two questions. As you worship and read the Scriptures, ask yourself these two questions: What does the gospel promise about God? And what do I need most from God in order to get through my loss? You already know the answer to the first question. The gospel promises God's abiding presence, care, concern, and provision. God remains *with* us, no matter what comes our way. You may find it helpful to remind yourself of what you know. You can do this by telling yourself something like this: "God is with me. God loves me. God will provide for me. In turn, I need to rely on God." Another approach may work better for you, but you get the idea. Sometimes, we need reminders of what we know about God in order to trust God and commit ourselves to God's care. If you don't feel that you know much about God, consider telling yourself what others (Bible, church, theologians, ministers, saints of the church) know about God's nature and desires. This may help you come to "know" God in a new and richer way.

As for the second question—What do I need most from God in order to get through my loss?—worship and reading Scripture can help you gain clarity about your needs. The idea is not to use these faith practices to manipulate God according to our desires or requirements. We don't commit to worship or reading Scripture, or any other faith practices, simply because doing so promises "rewards" for our lives. Plenty of people who dedicate their lives to God know that they receive no guarantee that what they ask of God will actually come to pass. We ask for healing, and people still die. We want reconciliation with spouses, and we still divorce. There is no magic in any faith practice. The goal of all faith practices is an encounter with God. We seek to "enjoy" God's presence. We seek after God for being God. It is as simple as that.

And yet, the Scriptures and Christian tradition are full of assurances with respect to two matters concerning God. First, God stays present in our lives and God provides. Recall Jesus' words to his disciples, "I will ask the Father, and he will give you another Advocate, to be with you forever. This is the Spirit of truth, whom the world cannot receive, because it neither sees him nor knows him. You know him, because he abides with you, and he will be in you" (John 14:16–17). Second, we may ask God to remain present and provide for us, and trust that God will do so. As Jesus urged in his Sermon on the Mount, "Ask, and it will be given you; search, and you will find; knock, and the door will be opened for you. For everyone who asks receives, and everyone who searches finds, and for everyone who knocks, the door will be opened" (Matt. 7:7–8).

Step 3: Practice steps 1 and 2 with at least one other person. Like almost any meaningful activity, worship and reading Scripture become more enriching and a part of us when practiced with others. Christian practices are meant to be engaged in with companions in faith. We may engage in them in solitude and find benefits in doing so. But we cannot practice the Christian faith entirely alone. We need others to live and enjoy the Christian story along with us. Others need us for the same reason. So along with attending Sunday or midweek services at your church, find ways to meet regularly with someone, or several persons, with whom you may read Scripture and ponder it together. This will bind you closer to the Christian story, God, and other people. This will likely help you mourn well.

Serving Others

Another faith practice to consider is serving others, or what we might call *hospitality*. Hospitality lies at the heart of the Christian story and its claim upon its devotees. Jesus' own life demonstrated that living in close relationship to God necessarily involves opening ourselves to others in lives of service. The book of Hebrews says as much, urging that we should "not neglect to show hospitality to strangers, for by doing that some have entertained angels without knowing it" (Heb. 13:2). We practice our faith by living hospitably, serving others as Jesus served.

We live hospitably out of faithfulness to the gospel. Our primary motivation is always to serve God by serving others. Once again, we don't practice hospitality as a means to some greater end. But practicing hospitality surely offers benefits, not only for the Christian life, but especially for mourning. Three benefits are described below.

We shift attention from ourselves to others. Serving others helps get your mind off yourself, at least for a while. This can prove helpful for mourning. Those who mourn find it difficult to divert their attention from themselves and their own situation. This follows not from selfishness but from the intense pain that loss brings. You focus on yourself when you suffer loss because it hurts so badly and you want the hurt to go away. You may become consumed by your loss and its effects because they *are* so intense and far-reaching.

Shifting your focus to others and their need offsets this tendency to focus too much on your own pain and needs. A focus on others also serves to alleviate *their* plight. You may offer them support, nurture, prayers, and helpful resources. At the same time, focusing on others relieves your *own* plight too, providing for what *you* need. You need rest from working so hard to provide for yourself. This rest may come as you seek to provide for others. And if you cannot provide for them, you can certainly journey with them as God provides.

This is not to suggest that you should stop attending to yourself and your needs as you mourn. This entire book has focused on how to pay close attention to yourself in the wake of a loss. But attending *only* to your needs, and focusing on yourself and your loss *exclusively*, may do more harm than good. All of us benefit from finding ways to shift our focus away from our plight, whatever its nature, so that we may find emotional and spiritual rest. So serve others because God has called you to serve them. But recognize that in serving others, you not only respond faithfully to God but you may lighten your own load too.

We experience solidarity in suffering. The apostle Paul urges the Christians in Galatia to "bear one another's burdens, and in this way you will fulfill the law of Christ" (Gal. 6:2). To walk with others in times of need is to suffer *with* them. This shared suffering reminds us of God's suffering with us. Sharing another's suffering also serves to remind us that we are not the only ones who suffer. This is true even when another's struggle differs from ours.

Becky has suffered for almost a decade since discovering that her adult son was missing. To my knowledge, she and her husband, Sam, still have had no word on his whereabouts, and they don't know whether he is dead or alive. As pastor to Becky and Sam for several years after their son went missing, I observed the anguish caused by living between hope and fear. They hoped that he'd soon call or be located by the private detective they hired, but they feared that they would learn that he had died or been killed. One can only imagine the pain of living with such uncertainty. I have witnessed both Becky and Sam drawing strength from people in their church during this time. In different ways, each has been lifted by the presence and prayers of the congregation. But during this time, Becky has made it her special mission to reach out to others in need. She has led a women's Bible study. She has regularly visited people in a local shelter and carried them donations made by people in the church. She has also spent significant time with ill and older persons, driving them to doctors' appointments or to other places they needed to go. She has also visited them on a regular basis, reminding them that they are important and that they still have something to contribute to others' lives.

Becky did these things before her son went missing, and before she lived with such pain. But she does more of these things now. I'm convinced that, in the midst of her own suffering, she finds peace, comfort, and probably hope as well, as she not only witnesses the suffering of others but seeks to share in their suffering. She indicated this to me once when she said, "There is so much pain in people's lives, and we need each other to get through it." She recognized that sharing others' burdens not only helps them, but may relieve our own burdens as well.

Solidarity in suffering may serve to relieve the pain of what theologian Jürgen Moltmann calls the "suffering in suffering" and "wounds in wounds."[6] This pain occurs when we think that our suffering lies beyond God's awareness or that of other people; it occurs, too, when we think that we alone suffer.

We gain confidence in God's presence and provision. We serve God by serving others. In serving God and others we live the Christian story. As we live this story our confidence in God's presence and provision increases. Why? Because in living the Christian story we witness how God sustains those who suffer. We meet those who suffer and observe them drawing strength, courage, and hope from what God provides. We also see how trusting in God's presence and provision buoys those who might otherwise collapse under the weight of their pain. Witnessing another person trust in God, rely upon God, and hope because of God may help us become more trustful, reliant, and hopeful ourselves. Don't underestimate the power of seeing God at work in others' lives for helping you see God at work in your own life.

8

So What Role Can Prayer Play?

The Scriptures speak often of prayer and its power. The same Scriptures encourage us to "pray without ceasing" (1 Thess. 5:17). The following passage from the Letter of James represents what the Bible says about prayer and its virtues:

> Are any among you suffering? They should pray. Are any cheerful? They should sing songs of praise. Are any among you sick? They should call for the elders of the church and have them pray over them, anointing them with oil in the name of the Lord. The prayer of faith will save the sick, and the Lord will raise them up; and anyone who has committed sins will be forgiven. Therefore confess your sins to one another, and pray for one another, so that you may be healed. The prayer of the righteous is powerful and effective. (James 5:13–16)

The sixteenth-century theologian John Calvin called prayer "the chief exercise of faith."[1] He recognized in the Christian faith the promise that God remains the source for what we need in life. This promise permits us to seek God, become better acquainted with God, and call upon God to provide. We do all of this through prayer.

We need to pray alone. As we know from the Gospels, Jesus did this. He "would withdraw to deserted places and pray" (Luke 5:16). But we must likewise pray with others. If we "pray without ceasing," we pray at all times, when we are alone and when we are with others.[2] In other words, we live constantly in a posture of prayer. Through praying, we grow and strengthen in relationship to God and others, much as our muscles and tissues grow and strengthen through physical exercise. As the "chief exercise of faith," prayer keeps us "fit" for living as God would have us be. Perhaps just as important, our "fitness" allows us to recover more quickly and completely when we sustain injury.

Prayer involves speaking to God and listening for God. Prayer draws us toward God's love, passion, and desire for all of creation, including ourselves. In prayer we may *internalize* God's presence and promise as conveyed by the writer in the book of Jeremiah, "I will turn their mourning into joy, I will comfort them, and give them gladness for sorrow" (Jer. 31:13). To "internalize" is a way of speaking about making something or someone a deep part of ourselves. When we internalize something, we believe it, trust it, and live in close relationship to it. It shapes our experiences because of the place it holds inside us. By virtue of being "in" us, it makes claims on us and how we live. Practicing prayer regularly results in our holding God's presence within our hearts and souls. We also hold fast to God's promise to abide with us, turning mourning into joy, offering comfort, and imparting gladness. Prayer unites us with God in unique and life-changing ways. It is the "chief exercise of faith."

WAYS OF PRAYING

There are more ways to approach prayer than any single book could sort out. Two ways of praying as you mourn, however, may be especially helpful. These include praying the Lord's Prayer and engaging in contemplative or quiet prayer. Let's consider these approaches briefly. Afterward, I suggest some steps for incorporating these and other ways of praying in your daily life.

The Lord's Prayer

Think about granting the Lord's Prayer a central place in your praying life. This puts you on solid biblical and historical ground. When Jesus' first followers asked that he teach them how to pray (Luke 11:1), he responded with what we now call the "Lord's Prayer." One common version of this familiar prayer goes like this:

Our Father in heaven,
  hallowed be your name,
  your kingdom come,
  your will be done,
    on earth as in heaven.
Give us today our daily bread.
Forgive us our sins
  as we forgive those who sin against us.
Save us from the time of trial
  and deliver us from evil.

For the kingdom, the power, and the glory are yours
  now and for ever. Amen.

This prayer addresses God and sets the basis of prayer in honoring God—"hallowed be your name." But this prayer also reminds us that as we address God and honor God we may ask God to provide what we need. In offering it as a model of prayer, Jesus implies that God hears us and acts on our behalf, according to our need. "Give us today our daily bread." "Forgive us our sins as we forgive the sins of others." "Save us from the time of trial." "Deliver us from evil." These requests cover much of what we need from God throughout life.

We benefit from God's offers of daily provision, forgiveness, and the capacity to forgive in times of loss. Likewise, we may need "saving" from all sorts of "trials" and "evils" that come our way in grief and mourning. These needs present themselves in different ways. Good mourning requires us to be aware of this and also to pray for our needs to be met accordingly. Gaining more familiarity with the Lord's Prayer and praying it regularly will foster this awareness and may contribute to your living a more prayerful life.

Contemplative Prayer

Another way to approach prayer is through contemplation or quiet reflection. The Roman Catholic tradition has spawned a method for this called "centering prayer." One of its foremost contemporary advocates, Thomas Keating, suggests that centering prayer aims to help "center" one's attention on God's presence.[3] Sometimes in prayer we attend to how God's presence affects *us*. At other times we attend to how God's presence affects others and the rest of creation. In both instances we focus on moving extraneous thoughts and feelings outside of our awareness. We seek to keep them there so that we can limit our attention to God's presence and lead.

Keating suggests a method for centering prayer. We will briefly consider his main points. First, get yourself in a comfortable position and place. Perhaps sitting in a room of your home or in a quiet place outdoors will work. Next, close your eyes. Then begin to let go of your collection of thoughts by thinking just one thought. Perhaps you are consumed with thoughts about the pain of your loss, your children's struggles, or how you will make ends meet financially now that you are a single parent. You probably have numerous other painful thoughts in your head, too.

In centering prayer, you want to find a way to move these painful thoughts outside of your immediate awareness, so that you can become more aware of God's presence and leading. Focusing on one thought, or one word, is a good way to do this. You might want your thought (word) to be "God" or "Jesus," or perhaps one of God's attributes, like "love," "mercy," "peace," "joy," "justice," or "grace." The word or image you settle on for this centering process is your choice. But it needs to become sacred for you. It represents your desire and intention to present yourself before God openly, so that you may experience the fullness of God's presence and nurture.

Once you have settled on the sacred word, allow it to enter your consciousness and claim a place there. Keating says it this way: "Introduce the sacred word into your imagination as gently as if you were laying a feather on a piece of absorbent cotton."[4] So invite the word into yourself, but don't force it or hold on to it too strongly. Simply allow it to reside with you on its own terms, whatever they are. Your goal here is not merely repetition of the word, but rather to allow the word to live in your imagination so that it points your attention toward God and the things of God. When you find yourself wandering from the word, thinking other thoughts or placing your energies in different matters, recall the sacred word. It will serve to draw you back, over and over again, to your open posture toward God's presence and promises.

We seek through centering prayer a state of "interior silence" or "rest in God." With these states come new emotional and spiritual places. These bring to mind the need to relocate losses in our emotional lives. In finding a place for what we have lost, we change our relationship to it. The loss "lives on" and we visit it when needed, but it no longer dominates our lives. It resides in a different emotional place, which provides relief from the pain of loss.

A state of interior silence or rest in God offers similar relief. Securing interior silence or rest in God transports us, emotionally, spiritually, and relationally. We move *from* the place where the pain of loss consumes us, and *to* a place where the pain becomes more manageable. Why? Because we have become more aware of God's presence, promise, and lead.

The Mercy Prayer

Another well-known Catholic writer, Henri Nouwen, offers a modified centering approach. It's called the "Mercy Prayer." When we experience life's difficulties and feel powerless to manage our pain, Nouwen suggests that we might commit ourselves to saying again and again, "Lord, have mercy." He writes,

> What are you to do? Make the conscious choice to move the attention of your anxious heart away from these waves [of anxiety] and direct it to the One who walks on them and says, "It's me. Do not be afraid" (Mt. 14:27; Mk. 6:50; Jn. 6:20). Keep turning your eyes to him and go on trusting that he will bring peace to your heart. Look at him and say, "Lord, have mercy." Say it again and again, not anxiously but with confidence that he is very close to you and will put your soul to rest.[5]

As we mourn, reminders that God offers mercy and that we may call upon God constantly to offer it to us may prove more sustaining than anything else.

You may discover that these two approaches to prayer help you find your way through loss with greater confidence and trust in God. Or perhaps these approaches, like the approach to praying the Lord's Prayer, will give you ideas for some other approach to prayer. What is important is not the way you pray but *that* you pray. Pray regularly in ways that prove meaningful to you, deepen your life of faith, and help you rely on God and others to get through your grief.

THREE STEPS FOR MAKING PRAYER
A CENTRAL PART OF YOUR LIFE

Here are three straightforward steps for incorporating prayer in your daily life. If you commit to them, you will discover a richer prayer life and greater sense of God's presence, comfort, and lead.

Step 1: Pray multiple times each day. Think about praying a *minimum* of three times a day, including when you awake, at lunch or in the early afternoon, and before you turn in for the night. This may sound excessive at first, especially if you currently spend little time in prayer. Furthermore, you may not be able to spend the same amount of time praying at each of these junctures. But attempt to spend at least a few minutes three times a day in prayer.

Perhaps you can begin with five minutes at a time, for a total of fifteen minutes in prayer each day. This need not be viewed as a rigid requirement, but only a suggested way to start. Like anything else that becomes part of your routine, the more you pray, the more you will miss *not* praying. The key is finding a way to begin your routine and then to stay with it.

In my view, the most important time to pray is in the morning. If you only engage in this "chief exercise of faith" once a day, do it when you first awake (or perhaps after your first cup of coffee!). But remember that the better approach will involve the "three or more times a day" method.

Bonhoeffer recognized the significance of beginning each day in a posture of prayer. He writes, "For Christians the beginning of the day should not be burdened and oppressed with besetting concerns for the day's work. . . . Therefore, at the beginning of the day let all distraction and empty talk be silenced and let the first thought and the first word belong to him to whom our whole life belongs."[6] Bonhoeffer knew that praying promotes an encounter with God and the Christian story.

If you decide to pray the Lord's Prayer, feel free to use the version cited here or any other that you appreciate. One approach might be to recite the prayer multiple times at each juncture of day that you pray. As you recite it, focus on the prayer's petitions individually, that is, each line that requests something of God. Take your time. The goal is not speed or getting finished so that you may move on to something else. Rather, the idea here is to seek deeper familiarity with what this prayer that Jesus offered as a model tells us about God, ourselves, and what we may ask God to provide. So savor each word and petition. Mull it over. Sit with it for a moment or two. Allow the words and their meaning to wash over you and absorb (internalize) them as you pray.

This may seem a bit foreign and awkward at first. But stay with it. Over time you will feel more a part of the Christian story and God's promises. You will sense, too, that these have become more a part of you. Internalizing the story and promise of the gospel will provide you with a larger measure of comfort, hope, and trust in God as you mourn.

Step 2: Ponder two questions. As you pray, think about the two questions suggested previously: What does the gospel promise about God? And what do I need most from God in order to get through my loss? If your approach is more contemplative, you may want to attend to these questions *after* you pray. But you may also find a way to remain conscious of them while you pray. You already know that the gospel promises God's abiding presence and care. God is *with you.* God cares for *you.* God will provide for *you.* Remind yourself of what you know.

Regarding the second question—What do I need most from God in order to get through my loss?—prayer may help you clarify your needs as it unites you with sources for meeting them. The sources, of course, are God and other persons. Remember that we don't pray as a means to some greater end. Our end is communion with God and the people of God. But the psalmist assures us that in praying to God we enjoy the benefits that God provides: "Bless the LORD, O my soul, and all that is within me, bless his holy name. Bless the LORD, O my soul, and do not forget all his benefits" (Ps. 103:1–2). The gospel invites us to offer up our needs to God with confidence that God hears us and provides for our benefit. Jesus himself said as much to the woman at the well and in his Sermon on the Mount: "If you knew the gift of God, and who it is that is saying to you, 'Give me a drink,' you would have asked him, and he would have given you living water" (John 4:10). So "Ask, and it will be given you" (Matt. 7:7).

Remember that Jesus' words don't suggest that we get all that we want, when we want it, how we want it, or with whom we want it just by virtue of asking it of God. Life does not work that way, even life centered in prayer. But the Lord's Prayer, like the Christian story as a whole, indicates that we may approach God with arms open expecting God to respond. So think about meditating on what you need as you pray. Pay attention to matters of daily provision, forgiveness, the capacity to forgive, and the trials and evils you face with your loss.

Step 3: Practice steps 1 and 2 with at least one other person. There is no substitute for solitary prayer. Jesus confirms as much by modeling this practice in his own life: "And after he had dismissed the crowds, he went up the mountain by himself to pray" (Matt. 14:23). But if we limit ourselves to praying alone, we miss out on sharing faith with others. When the Bible says to "pray without ceasing," this means that we need to pray alone *and* with others in community.

You will find your own way to pray with others. One possibility might be to set a time at least once a week for meeting with one or two people (more if you like) to pray. Some approaches to prayer may lend themselves better than others to praying communally. For example, you may find it easier to pray with others using the Lord's Prayer, rather than praying with others contemplatively. Most Christian traditions include the Lord's Prayer in their worship services, for good reason. Whatever forms you choose, it's wonderful when prayer happens with others in the faith community. Faith practices can be engaged by ourselves *and* with others.

A BRIEF EXERCISE

It might be helpful for you to pause here. As you do, assume a posture of prayer. As you pray, discern how you will make prayer a more central part of your life. Don't worry. You need not have clear answers, and you certainly need not figure it all out. Simply begin a more intentional process of discovering a life of prayer. Spend five minutes praying the Lord's Prayer. Or, if you prefer, try a more contemplative approach or some other way of praying that you find meaningful. If you do this for five minutes and feel like staying with it longer, do it. The only way to understand prayer, become more familiar with it, and make it part of your life of faith is by doing it. How about doing it now?

Epilogue

Many people who experience a significant loss say that it changes their lives forever. Perhaps you would agree. For most of us, our *reality* is altered when we have loved someone or something deeply and then experience its loss. Life becomes different as we attempt to find our way through our pain. I have suggested that the Christian story offers some help for the journey. As the Christian story draws us into itself, we discover a different type of reality. It is the reality of God's transforming and redemptive work in human lives and all of creation through the life, death, and resurrection of Jesus and the ongoing work of the Holy Spirit.

Living with this reality affects how we experience loss. What we have loved is still gone. We continue to hurt in its absence. We long to be reunited with it. Our loss is felt differently, however, because we are more confident that God is with us. We trust that God will be a faithful companion on our journey through loss. We also hold fast to the hope that loss does not have the final word. Instead, God has the final word, and God promises to abide. Dietrich Bonhoeffer reminds us of *this* reality. He writes of suffering,

> A change has come indeed. Your hands, so strong and active, are bound; in helplessness now you see your action is ended; you sigh in relief, your cause committing to stronger hands; so now you may rest contented. Only for one blissful moment could you draw near to touch freedom; then, that it might be perfected in glory, you gave it to God.[1]

Perhaps we describe the Christian faith best when we say that it has everything to do with giving our pain to God. This is its reality. Experiencing the reality of the Christian story, its promises, and its hope, makes a difference in how we feel, think, and act. "Half-stitched scars" remain. Sometimes they still open to expose our wound afresh. When this happens, however, God and others with whom we share faith are ready to help us close them, and allow them to heal once more. As the prophet Jeremiah assures us on God's behalf: "I will turn their mourning into joy, I will comfort them, and give them gladness for sorrow" (Jer. 31:13). May God so comfort and bring gladness to you.

Appendix

*Combined List of Strategies for Coping
with Grief and Mourning Well*

Remember that these overlap with one another, may be redundant in
some ways, and that none necessarily is more important than any of the
others.

STRATEGIES FOR COPING WITH GRIEF

- Rehearse the events associated with learning about your loss in as much
  detail as you can tolerate.
- Place yourself in the presence of reminders of what you have lost.
- Recognize the value of funerals, and participate in them.
- Remind yourself that your feelings are natural and acceptable.
- Express yourself.
- Talk about your experience with a friend, a family member, or both.
- Talk about your experience with a minister, a counselor, or a spiritual
  director.
- Welcome your tears.
- Surround yourself with people, places, and activities that you enjoyed
  before your loss occurred.
- Seek the presence of those who comfort you.
- Place yourself in physical settings that offer comfort.
- Engage in other activities that offer comfort, rest, and promote recovery.
- Engage in moderate exercise and physical activity.
- Remember your errors, but do not allow them to consume you.
- Work on forgiving and being reconciled.

- Focus on the present, not the future.
- Recognize your pain as significant but not insurmountable.

STRATEGIES FOR GOOD MOURNING

- Tell yourself repeatedly that your loss has occurred (acknowledgment) and also that you need to go forward living with the void it has left (acceptance).
- Make use of rituals that encourage confronting your loss.
- Seek support from your minister, faith community, and others who care for you.
- Dare to be alone.
- Continue to identify your feelings, thoughts, and behaviors, but now assign them a value.
- Identify changes you need to make to adapt to your loss, but prioritize them.
- Cultivate a "place" for what you have lost.
- Consider the benefits of new opportunities, interests, roles, relationships, and goals that present themselves.
- Remind yourself that you will mourn in ways distinctly your own.
- Seek to deepen your faith in God and God's provision.

Notes

Introduction

1. Elizabeth Jennings, "Words about Grief," in *Collected Poems* (New York: Carcanet, 1986).
2. Dorothy S. Becvar, *In the Presence of Grief: Helping Family Members Resolve Death, Dying, and Bereavement Issues* (New York: Guilford Press, 2001).

Chapter 1: What Makes Loss So Difficult?

1. John Bowlby, *Attachment and Loss*, vol. 1, 2nd ed. (1969; repr., New York: Basic Books, 1982).
2. Nicholas Wolterstorff, *Lament for a Son* (Grand Rapids: Wm. B. Eerdmans, 1987), 55.

Chapter 3: What Effect Does Loss Have on How We Think and Behave?

1. In some Native American cultures, and possibly some others, it is customary to burn or otherwise quickly destroy or remove clothing of the deceased from the home. In that case, this can be considered a valid response to loss.

Chapter 4: What Helps Us Cope with Loss?

1. I am grateful to my colleague David Lee Jones for pointing out the origins of the word *hearse* and suggesting that I think about the relationship between "rehearsing" and "harrowing." See Susan I. Spitz, ed., *Webster's II New College Dictionary*, 3rd ed. (Boston: Houghton Mifflin, 2005), s.v. "hearse."
2. William Shakespeare, *Macbeth*, 4.3.
3. Alfred Lord Tennyson, "In Memoriam A. H. H," in *Tennyson's Poetry: Authoritative Texts, Juvenilia and Early Responses, Criticism*, ed. Robert W.

Hill Jr., Norton Critical Edition (New York: W. W. Norton and Co., 1971), 122.

Chapter 5: So What Does Mourning Require?

1. These five features of mourning are based on the four "tasks" of mourning as considered by J. William Worden. Worden's tasks include: accept the reality of the loss; work through the pain of grief; adjust to the environment in which the deceased is missing; and emotionally relocate the deceased and move on with life. See *Grief Counseling and Grief Therapy: A Handbook for the Mental Health Practitioner*, 3rd ed. (New York: Springer Publishing Co., 2005).
2. Allan Hugh Cole Jr., "Monday Mourning: Negotiating Losses in Retirement," *Presbyterian Outlook* 189, no. 25 (July 30/August 6, 2007): 11.

Chapter 6: So What Promotes Good Mourning?

1. J. William Worden says that mourning requires the fulfillment of tasks. This task-oriented approach centers on mourners "doing" particular things—namely, completing tasks—to facilitate their mourning.

Chapter 7: So What Role Can Faith Play?

1. For a fuller treatment of how thinking about the Christian faith in this way relates to various faith practices, see Allan Hugh Cole Jr., *Be Not Anxious: Pastoral Care of Disquieted Souls* (Grand Rapids: Wm. B. Eerdmans, forthcoming).
2. Dietrich Bonhoeffer, *Letters and Papers from Prison*, ed. Eberhard Bethge (1953; repr., New York: Touchstone, 1977), 360–61.
3. Dietrich Bonhoeffer, *Life Together: The Classic Exploration of Life in Community*, trans. John W. Doberstein (New York: HarperSanFrancisco, 1954), 53–54.
4. This list comes from Claus Westermann, *The Psalms: Structure, Content, and Message* (Minneapolis: Augsburg, 1980), 53.
5. Dietrich Bonhoeffer, *Life Together/Prayerbook of the Bible*, in *Dietrich Bonhoeffer Works*, vol. 5, ed. Geffrey B. Kelly; trans. Daniel W. Bloesch and James H. Burtness; gen. editor, Wayne Whitson Floyd (1996; repr., Minneapolis: Fortress Press, 2005).
6. Jürgen Moltmann, *The Crucified God* (1974; repr., Minneapolis: Fortress Press, 1993), 46.

Chapter 8: So What Role Can Prayer Play?

1. John Calvin, *Institutes of the Christian Religion*, vol. 2, ed. John T. McNeill, trans. Ford Lewis Battles (Philadelphia: Westminster Press, 1960), 850.
2. For an excellent book on prayer and praying, see Deborah van Deusen Hunsinger, *Pray without Ceasing: Revitalizing Pastoral Care* (Grand Rapids: Wm. B. Eerdmans, 2006).
3. See Thomas Keating, *Open Mind Open Heart: The Contemplative Dimension of the Gospel* (1986; repr., New York: Continuum, 2006), especially pp. 109–15.

4. Ibid., 110.

5. Henri J. M. Nouwen, *The Inner Voice of Love: A Journey through Anguish to Freedom* (1996; repr., New York: Doubleday, 1998), 98.

6. Dietrich Bonhoeffer, *Life Together: The Classic Exploration of Life in Community*, trans. John W. Doberstein (New York: HarperSanFrancisco, 1954), 43.

Epilogue

1. Dietrich Bonhoeffer, *Letters and Papers from Prison*, ed. Eberhard Bethge (1953; repr., New York: Touchstone, 1957), 371.

For Further Reading

LeRoy Aarons, *Prayers for Bobby: A Mother's Coming to Terms with the Suicide of Her Gay Son*

Judi Benson and Agneta Falk, eds., *The Long Pale Corridor: Contemporary Poems of Bereavement*

Leo Buscaglia, *The Fall of Freddie the Leaf*

John Claypool, *Tracks of a Fellow Struggler*

Greg Garrett, *Stories from the Edge: A Theology of Grief*

Earl Grollman, *What Helped Me When My Loved One Died*

Matthew Levering, ed., *On Christian Dying: Classic and Contemporary Texts*

C. S. Lewis, *A Grief Observed*

Thomas Lynch, *The Undertaking: Life Studies from the Dismal Trade*

Mary Jane Moffatt, *In the Midst of Winter: Great Writers Express the Inexpressible*

Henri J. M. Nouwen, *A Letter of Consolation*

———, *In Memoriam*

———, *The Only Necessary Thing: Living a Prayerful Life*

Sherwin B. Nuland, *How We Die: Reflections on Life's Final Chapter*

Therese A. Rando, *How to Go On Living When Someone You Love Dies*

Merton P. Strommen and A. Irene Strommen, *Five Cries of Grief*

R. Scott Sullender, *Grief and Growth*

Barry Ulanov, ed., *On Death: Wisdom and Consolation from the World's Great Writers*

Judith Viorst, *Necessary Losses: The Loves, Illusions, Dependencies, and Impossible Expectations That All of Us Have to Give Up in Order to Grow*

Andrew J. Weaver and Howard W. Stone, eds., *Reflections on Grief and Spiritual Growth*

Granger Westberg, *Good Grief*

Nicholas Wolterstorff, *Lament for a Son*

Revised Common Lectionary Resources

See Devotions and Readings, PC(USA), http://www.pcusa.org/devotions/
lectionary/index.htm.

See The Revised Common Lectionary, Vanderbilt Divinity Library, http://
divinity.library.vanderbilt.edu/lectionary.